THERE'S MORE TO YOU

Your Career Unveiled:
10 Essential Strategies to Master Your
Career, Business, and Life

by
Vanessa Guzman-Schepis

Published 2020

DISCLAIMER

ISBN (Print Book): 978-1-7343528-1-8

For me.
Or anyone who wrote notes on air or has curly hair.

Table of Contents

Chapter 1:
The Monday Morning Struggles

"A ship is always safe at shore, but that is not what it's built for."
– Albert Einstein

Admit it. At times you dread the thought of waking up to face the reality of work and life. We all do. Imagine this: It's Sunday. You're in bed, and as you doze off, you make a mental note not to forget to send an email about that project that keeps giving you a headache. Monday rolls in, and your journey begins. You get up, get out of bed you brush your teeth, take a shower, kids are still in bed, but you know they have to get up, and they are going to torment you because they don't want to get up, and it's only their third week in the school year! You walk to the kitchen, where it's nice and quiet, and you start the coffee. You know you need your coffee. It's October, and it's getting darker outside. The dog walks behind you, looking for its breakfast, ready to be walked. Of course, you're still trying to wake up. Your stomach starts aching, a typical Monday morning feeling.

You say to yourself, "Do I have to do this every day? There has to be more to life." You sit in your living room, and you take a deep breath. Is it boredom? Or are you stressed? Or do you feel tired? It must be the crazy busy weekend you've just had. You tell yourself the usual: It's going to be okay, you'll get in the car, drive to work, drop the kids off in school, and you'll feel better. The day won't get the best of you, and once you finish that report that's been dragging, all your problems will be lifted away from your shoulders.

You look at the clock, and you still have twenty extra minutes before you have to get the kids up, prepare lunch for everyone, and get ready. You take a deep breath, lay down on your sofa, close your eyes, and follow your breath as you've been told to do. Then, you start going over your list – the list of chores, that is. Let's see … scheduling your parents' doctor appointments, and the car is due for inspection (it's had the light on for some time), going to the bank, picking up groceries – wait, maybe I can get that through Amazon…not in the mood….

You realize you're not supposed to be thinking about your to-do list – that's not the point of meditating! You try again. You start by visualizing your happy place. You're on a beautiful beach, you hear the waves, you feel warmth of the sun touching your arms, caressing your face, you hear the birds chirping and the wind blowing softly. Oh, no – the coffee! You get up frantically, hoping that you have just one more minute.

As you beg the kids to get out of bed, you start reminiscing on what life has been to you for the last twenty years. Something is different about this morning. It's like the world is trying to communicate with you just a little differently today. You start remembering your college years, when you had dreams of owning a business, helping others, but you never were super sure exactly how to get there. So you figured getting a BA was general enough to get a job. College years were great; part of being young allowed you not to fear what you didn't know. At an early age, you were taught that you go to college, you make some money, you get a job, you meet the perfect person, you have kids, you buy a house, and you'll be fine. But then you find, twenty years later, that's not the case. Oh, wait. it's what you did precisely, but why aren't you excited when you get up in the morning? "I'm so tired", you now think to yourself.

You look back, and you realize that you made a series of decisions that somehow led you to where you are today. It's not like you're unhappy or ungrateful, but there's a yucky feeling that something's off. You wonder, "What's the purpose? I do the same things, every single day, I go to work, one of the kids gets sick in school, I have to pick them up, come back home, and the house is a mess." You know how that can go! Then you start dinner, and you try to get the kids to shower…(good luck).

Daydreaming

Your daydreaming, or more accurately, your spiraling, goes something like this: "I still have at least ten more years to raise my kids to spend time with them. It's hard to imagine us living off of one income. If I make the change and I don't like it, what will I wind up doing? I'm having a hard time imagining what exactly it is that I want to do, since it's been such a long time since I started working at this company. I don't know what I would do outside of it. I'm afraid that I'd feel lost because I've been doing the same thing now for almost twenty years, and I feel like it's the only thing I know how to do. I feel stagnant, almost like, 'What's the point of being there if every day feels like a struggle, the days are long?' I just have this nagging feeling in my insides that make me unhappy with myself. Not only is the commute very long, but I spend so many hours away from my family that I worry that I'm missing out on just spending time with the kids, enjoying my husband, and having the energy to do what it is that we love doing. I've lost touch with myself and even my friendships. By the time I get home, I'm exhausted. Although I have close friends, I barely have the time to spend time with them. I would love to go and travel all over the world. But can we afford it? Do we have enough time to take off? We don't make that type of money. We own a home, but with that comes a lot of expenses too."

Another thing that has become very, very tricky is the fact that both of your parents are aging fairly quickly. It's scary to think that one day, you, too, will reach that age where you are so dependent on your children (if they bother to care, of course). Your parents are no longer comfortable making decisions. So who else will do it? It has to be you.

At this point, you don't even know where this feeling is coming from. Your best friend has recently been diagnosed with cancer, and so you are in pieces, devastated, thinking the worst. Who would have imagined this would happen to her, since she's so young? One thing you realized was how fragile life is. You also realized that you hadn't done much with your life. A blindfold fell from your face, and all of a sudden, you saw your brief time on the planet for what it is.

Is This It?

So, it hits you: "What should I start doing now to get out of this data nonsense? Will I be making the same or more money, or should I start entry-level again, since it's been such a long time of working in the company? I don't know if I will be able to retain the same amount of information the way I used to in my twenties. When would I have time to learn something new? I might be too old even to start this. Yet, my biggest fear is missing out on the window of opportunity that I feel I have now. I can't bear the thought of having this regret ten years from now and saying to myself I could have done that. If I continue going down this path, what type of example would I be giving my kids? I feel like my husband doesn't get the full me. I need to understand what it is that I want to do with my life, with this job."

You arrive at work. Same drama. If someone were to ask you if you're having fun right now, you'd say point-blank "no". You feel you probably should have gone home after dropping the car off, instead of making the sacrifice of coming in to work. Maybe it is a lack of appreciation, or simply not seeing the value that you're receiving from your job. Again, you wonder if this is it. For years now, you've spent more time complaining about your job than embracing or learning newly found values and functions.

A change is imminent. Change is a constant in our lives, and one must embrace it. At this point in your life, it's becoming critical, for yourself and your family, to shift direction, or you will be at risk of feeling resentment toward yourself and others. It's not fair to those around you, especially your husband and kids, that as each day passes, you are miserable. You build yourself up to have better days, but honestly, it's no longer working for you. You know you need a change, but where do you start, and where should you go? It will take time, effort, and execution of a sound strategy to make the transition a reality.

One of the most difficult nuts to crack in life is how to remain happy or to achieve happiness with your situation. I'll start by stating: There isn't a secret sauce for career success. Instead, it becomes a series of things you enjoy, are good at, and see as valuable or enjoyable to others. Most of us will not achieve the riches and fame of Beyoncé, Bill Gates, or the Obamas. That's okay. They are pretty amazing if you ask me, and I'm thrilled each one is in our world. However, many of us do share the attributes or experiences that make them so, so special. I think they all achieved a unique path that belongs to them. Regardless of the chaos we often see in the world, I believe people genuinely carry a persona and a place in that world. It's not about whether that's good or bad. But instead, it's about acting and being as we were designed to be. Anything less is quite a loss. Striving to be the next someone else sets us up for great disappointment.

Instead, we should all be trying to find our paths. The first step is believing there is indeed a path for you. You are designed perfectly for *you*. Your design is tailored to match the changes throughout your lifetime. Many of the stories, advice, actions, and steps that I'll be sharing in this book come purely from a place of acknowledgment that there isn't one way of being amazing; but, more importantly, that you can be confident that *you are all you need* in life to be successful. No, I'm not trying to amp you up to then see you fail. I've been where you are, and I'm here to help by sharing my journey. So read on!

Chapter 2:
Seeking Career Happiness

"The future was uncertain, absolutely, and there were many hurdles, twists, and turns to come, but as long as I kept moving forward, one foot in front of the other, the voices of fear and shame, the messages from those who wanted me to believe that I wasn't good enough, would be stilled."
— Chris Gardner, *The Pursuit of Happyness (2016)*

My story is similar to many, I think. Nothing exciting, you'd say. And by the way, I'm in no way, shape, or form done with my journey.

Desiring a life with recognition as a reward and not-so-random encounters with resources opened the door to opportunities and a wealth of information about myself that would eventually shed light on my career path. Balancing a career with other areas of my life has been a tricky subject. Either my focus on my career development led to me ignore everything else, or I felt that if I didn't do enough or the way my parents taught me, I wouldn't merit the badge of successful. Then I was told that it was vital for me to work on myself.

Well, what does that mean exactly? It involves understanding your core values, recognizing and appreciating your talents and strengths, and then doing something about it. Let me tell you about myself. I'm no more or less unique than the soul reading this book. I'm busy; I have big and small issues, relationships that don't work, and health is not always on my side. But I'm grateful for my life, the expected and not intended, the people who were seasonal and those who are stuck with me for life. I'm thankful for you, my dear reader. I believe you will get precisely what you need from this book – whether you know it now or realize it later on.

Growing up Guzman

At a very young age, I would describe myself as curious, daring, one of the quiet ones that you should probably worry about. I was born in Brooklyn, New York, during the less hip era. During the eighties and nineties, New York was being dogged by a well-earned reputation for high crime rates, drugs, and violence. Like most immigrant Caribbean families during that time, my parents decided to move back to their native home, the Dominican Republic. It was their way of saving their kids from corrupt gangs and street life.

I remember being six years old, leaving our Brooklyn apartment in Park Slope along with my sister, who was twelve at the time, headed to what used to be our usual vacation destination. Except this time, it was a bit more permanent. It's where I learned how much I enjoyed alone time, enjoying nature. It was the only time I was able to think and play out scenes of numbers and characters. During bedtime, I would fall asleep, writing phrases and numbers on air. My sister was at the center of my life. In my mind, I would play a theme song of a sitcom when she was around or entered the room. She was very well liked. She was more like others in my family. The reason I bring this up is because, at an early age, I knew that I was different than most of my family members, even my culture. I was okay with that. It wasn't until my late teens that, like many, I started trying to blend in. Unfortunately, there was too little of myself that I liked to be able to blend in and still be myself. Growing up Guzman, became a combination of childhood growth, cultural ties and family wounds. Wounds that originated from prior generations and now being passed on to us, from a place of love but also insecurities and self-doubt.

Unique Wiring

Academically, I was labeled as high performing, requiring little study and acing most, if not all subjects. I quickly was in the honor roll and was president of my classes in grade school. My parents were very proud; high academic achievement was always celebrated in our home. It was our path to future successes in life. However, celebrations can also create wounds. One day, the class took a math exam. I scored a sixty-six. I rushed to the bathroom and cried as if I had lost a loved one. Crazy! Crazy talk! I think about it now and remain in awe how much that meant to me. The reason why it was so important was because my brain was my thing. The only thing prized and celebrated was for the first time was failing me. Although it can be painful, it's essential to acknowledge the moments one might remember from our childhood, as these can house our wounds today. Unresolved traumas, gratifications and experiences during our childhood start the formation of insecurities, needs and perceptions encountered during our adulthood.

On another day, my parents were driving me to an award ceremony. We were discussing what the award was for, and at some point, during the conversation, I told them that I would accomplish anything I wanted. "Vanessa will get whatever she wants," I said. They both looked at me, surprised, but also mumbling how much "trouble" I was, in a loving way, "This girl is out of her mind", not sure what made me so confident to say or respond with those words.

But today, I truly believe and stand by that statement, in the humblest ways. Not just for me. As I stated earlier in the book, we each have a path, and we can create and see a million reasons why we will not believe that; however, we can also choose to see the infinite opportunities we have if we're willing to use them. For each thought, action, and outcome, there's a perspective and response. As a child, I was awarded several recognitions, medals, certificates for high performance, or participating in competitions. One may think that's great. One day, I sincerely would love to see my children being the best they can be at whatever that will be. In my case, the result of often being rewarded for my efforts was that, as a young adult, I had hoped others would see them. I've always thrived on achievement and completion. But apart from that, desiring affirmation and support from the world is different. That feeling of being liked, accepted, and needed is what for years fueled my desire to be better. It was the culprit of unfulfilling relationships, not just with people, but between me and myself. The same girl that thought she would always get what she wanted, also felt she had to please others. On one side, this orientation left me with great humility, detachment from the material, and the heart of a giver. However, on the flip side, my actions were primarily driven by attempting to meet someone else's desires.

According to Perceptions

On a separate note, like many people, my weight has been a subject of attention. Usually for "lack of" that is. I was always on the slimmer side. In the Dominican culture, and certainly in my home, women with fuller, curvier figures were often subject to admiration. I, on the other hand, have what's commonly referred to as a straight or athletic body shape. When I look at pictures from my childhood, I don't see that. I had terrific-looking cheeks and certainly had a very healthy weight. Still, as part of my diet, my mom would give me appetite enhancing vitamins to make sure I looked fuller. My legs were too skinny, she thought, and I tended to look "sick."

So the well-nourished weight that I now see in the pictures was the result of induced weight gain. I remember looking at myself and not being pleased with how I felt, and feeling hungry when I had just had a meal. For weeks, I would sleep with a belt tied around my waist, hoping to be slimmer, as I was later. I would look at other girls, both those thinner and more substantial, and think to myself, "They seem happy, so how come I can't be happy?" There were days when I was called "transparent" in Spanish, referring to being "see-through", too skinny or thin. I would try to control the portions I would eat or pretend to eat all the food my mom would give me, but it would be hard to manage to control your weight when the vitamins would kick in. For years, I would stay away from wearing shorts because I thought that my legs were too skinny. Note that I lived in a tropical country, so this was extremely difficult.

It was a constant tug of war between how my family and others expected I would look like, and what my body was telling me was right for me at that time. People are not only mocked for being overweight, but for any feature not aligned with that norm or others' expectations. The lesson learned here is that my body is precisely that; it is *my* body. Its ideal state is one of health, with the ability to carry my life to support my spirit, thoughts, and actions.

One day, my seventh-grade teacher asked the class what we considered to be an essential part of our body. I answered my hands and brain, thinking they had carried me so far. One would describe me as nerdy or weird, but I did always appreciate my brain's wiring. It had given me many rewards in life, not to mention that I could understand that I would see things very differently than others. Still, as an adult, I can see the future more clearly when my present is focused, decluttered from all the noise that exists. I also have an eye for opportunities. Not to say I'm psychic or predict how the stock market will perform – I would certainly have a very different career path if that were the case. But from an early age, I would connect things, whether those were ideas, thoughts, and especially numbers. It's no surprise that I would wind up in a career in science, medicine, or engineering. This example illustrates how looking back at one's childhood, often provides clues to our nature, untampered state and the source of values and behavior.

Numbers and Quotas

I thought confrontation and standing up for what I believed in, could only come from a place of anger. Instead, the opportunity stands strong when acts of love, kindness and compassion come along with your message. That's the real lesson.

Who do I need to apologize to? Consider it done!",
although I didn't feel like it.

While the kids were playing in the backyard, I would
be daydreaming. Imagining sitting at my desk as an adult,
giving my clients plans, like architectural designs and
floor plans. Plans containing numbers, graphics and a
wealth of information. Numbers have always been some
of my best friends. They speak to me like no other human
can communicate with me. In high school, I rarely had to
study for math or science exams; during the tests, I felt
like the digits spoke to me and re-arranged themselves to
form the perfect sequence, equations, and outputs.

Junior and senior years were all about the college. I
believed your degree would define the rest of your career,
your life, one could say. My friends and I would spend
plenty of time in the college office. Applying for scholarships and searching for schools that would accept me
became probably the primary topic of discussion. To encourage healthy competition, but also recognition among
its students, our school asked us to post our total scholar-
ship monetary awards at the lobby entrance. It helped us
aspire to get as many scholarships and college applica-
tions out the door as possible. For weeks, I was number
one on the bulletin. My teammates, who were serious
competitors, were listed as well. Amid the celebrations
and competition, one of the top performers pointed out
that I and others were being accepted to schools and ob-
taining these scholarships because the schools were looking to meet their "quota", referring to affirmative action.
(Reader, I'm not going into the specifics of affirmative
action in this book, but this, among many programs and
policies, aims to position underserved or underprivileged

groups, by considering race a factor for college admissions. It's not strictly a quota-based system.)

A few of us felt genuinely hurt by the comment, thinking to ourselves that these schools weren't just picking anyone from the streets; we were still as high achieving as anyone else. It was the first time that my merit and achievement felt undermined. My best friend at the time and I decided to retaliate. I think of that now, and boy, oh, boy, did I have chops! But we wanted to be classy. We each had to write an essay and read out loud during our Advanced Placement English class. We decided to write a poem and share the stage. The poem described our experience as undermined, high achieving Hispanics being targeted by two other girls, who were using their power to lessen the value of other students and were worried about missing out on opportunities.

The entire class and the teacher were appalled. I remember tears and quickly being called to the gym teacher's office. My best friend and I were asked to apologize, given that the delivery of the message was not necessary, and to acknowledge that we had hurt other teammates in the process. My best friend insisted that we were the victims of the offense, and the girls were not worthy of an apology. I was a total chicken and quickly thought to myself, "I don't want this to be in my records. Who do I need to apologize to? Consider it done!", although I didn't feel like it.

At that point, it was apparent to me that the determination of merit was a complicated subject, one that my efforts alone would no longer control. Not only did I have to depend on others to celebrate and recognize my achievements, but my results were now going to be subject to evaluation based on social and physical factors that were given to me at birth. One factor was having people, systems, and processes facilitate a step; another was the value and the action I placed on the challenge. The result of this situation: that fall, I was accepted to one of the most prestigious schools in the country and was off to confront new-found challenges. This story represents not only the complexities of our world as universal culture, but of beliefs and values sometimes shaken when we lack understanding of our *own* being and core values.

Hello, World

At the time, I considered studying computer engineering. "Hello, world.", a standard output in computer language program, represented more than just a language but a reflection of the exposure to an unknown to the world ahead of me. The summer of 2003 was probably one of the most complex, life-changing experiences I had ever had. Leaving home to go away for school was perhaps the biggest culture shock experienced by me and my family. (Many such moments ensued, as you'll learn later in the book.) I remember my mom asking me if I was sure I wanted to go to that school, because it might be too hard.. This is what I consider a "blind spot". It's a term I use more and more as I heal the relationship with my parents, in particular, my mom. I respect them, but find it hard to understand my parents when they emphasize or prioritize hardship and external perception, over will-power. It's the battle between our worlds and upbringing. That being said, I gladly went ahead and packed up my things, and my parents dropped me off.

I must say, however, that I was then about forty-five minutes from home by NYC subway. This is a joke to many, including myself, now. But back then, although part of me felt it was natural for me to go away and grow, my innards were tying me to my upbringing, my roots, the things that were important to me. All I had was my parents and my sister, and now I was moving? I must have no heart, no soul. Remarks made earlier that year also made me question whether or not I was worthy of being there among the best. Was it indeed a favor, or did I have the brains to belong? I must admit, the coursework was brutal.

Whether it was a lack of confidence or simply adjusting to college life, I was not performing as well as I wanted to. I would go home every weekend, because that's what my parents expected and what made them happy. As a result, I didn't have much time to focus on the coursework and on collaborating with my friends, or going to parties and just having plain fun as a young student in one the most vibrant cities in the world. It felt more like a Goodbye, World, than it certainly felt like Hello. I wasn't able to find a midpoint between being a good daughter and being a good student and or just being kind to myself.

I was having a challenging time focusing on and finding my place. It was the first time I felt the need to work to achieve my desired outcomes. In the past, this was much more manageable. What happened to me, I wondered? Ultimately, I took three semesters off school and started seeing a therapist. This is an example of how life may change its course, to allow the opportunity to address barriers that may challenge one further if left unattended. Sometimes, this requires a pause, perhaps coaching or being challenged differently all together, to move into uncharted territory and closer to a greater version of oneself.

Messing with My Psyche

Even now, my family doesn't know that I sought help at that time. At the mention of psychiatric or mental help, my family often uses the term "crazy" to refer to those who seek it. But at that point in my life, I felt that I couldn't solve the problem on my own. I was stuck, with no way out. I was impulsive. I also developed a habit of lying at every opportunity I would find. It's almost as though my life wasn't entertaining enough, so it needed improvisation for others to be fascinated by it. So…let's make up a story. How would I succeed in school if I couldn't focus? Let's take shortcuts. The therapist never fully diagnosed me but said I was displaying many symptoms of those with ADHD, borderline, or bipolar disorder. Specific, right? No. I stopped seeing her eventually, since I could not find the way to effectively implement the suggestions she would make, like talking to my parents or following a plan in school to help me stay focused. Instead, I thought, it would be easier to leave therapy.

Eventually, I went back to school, without being given a care plan or treated with medication (something I might consider doing differently today). I remember being home and, one day, buying a pack of cigarettes, opening the window, and blowing out a very unpleasant inhale of Marlboro. Never again did I smoke.

For me, the lesson here is that bad behavior leads to more bad behavior. The place where you are attracts more of the same influences. Not addressing feelings, whether it is of anger, confusion, loss, or depression, will manifest in more ways than one, and, usually, more aggressively and impactfully as these feelings accumulate. The opposite is also accurate. Being in a state of inner harmony attracts opportunities, abundance, and other things that are right for you.

Kicking Myself into Gear

I went back to school and started working for a lab. At the same time, I was doing an internship in economics, offered to me as I was debating whether or not I would change majors. The timing was perfect. I felt that I would again be in a position of control after coming out of severe confusion and lack of confidence, and beginning to question my purpose. This enabled me the opportunity, not only to earn money, but to once again feel good at something. For a very long time, I had felt lost. Oh, it was almost like I had created a different person over the last two years, who now needed to work herself out.

Soon after completing the internship, I gravitated toward the field of medicine. One thing I knew for sure was my desire to help others. As a child, I had adopted from my parents the sense of community and sharing – be it your wealth, time, or other material goods – with other people who are in need. At that point in my educational path, I thought to myself that it would be an excellent opportunity to become an emergency medical technician (EMT). I would see the EMT students taking care of intoxicated colleagues in the middle of the night, and I found that prospect fascinating. So, during my transition back to school, I decided to enroll in an EMT course in my local neighborhood. The intent all along was to practice it while I was in school. I loved it!

The following summer, after getting my certification as an EMT, I decided to formalize my training by joining the Fire Department of the City of New York. I thought it would be "real" if I could see patients in my community and obtain direct experience. It would help me decide whether the field of healthcare, or patient care, were areas worth pursuing. I remember doing the last few days of academy training, when we had the opportunity to select where we would want to work. From a pool of students, the faculty chose your location based on your last name. That somehow played out favorably, and I was able to work in Harlem. That would have enabled me to continue going to school and also work full time. I now felt empowered, more like myself. I thought I was achieving.

What I didn't know is that work would start being my escape from what continued to occur inside of me. I was very unhappy with myself, but thought that things would get better in the ways that I knew how to get them better. That meant through work. I now know that taking a closer look at our intent, when we gravitate towards our career, jobs, relationships or any use of our time, surfaces our agendas, and gives us the opportunity to perform an alignment check against our life's true agenda.

Oh, Boy, Oh, Boys...

It was during my employment as an EMT that I met the man who, three years later, became my first husband. I was twenty years old at the time. My sister was close to getting married, and things were quickly changing back at home. I started feeling like I needed to go back to the social norms; it seemed less complicated. It was the first time I started thinking to myself, "Why was I so happy during my childhood and not so much now? Is it because I'm away from my parents? Is it because I won't have the same relationship with my sister now that she's getting married? Is it because of my job? I feel tired all the time." But somehow, the idea of getting married seemed to be the right thing to do, as I was approaching my last year in graduate school.

I had decided to pursue a career in biomedical engineering, and to seek a corporate job that best suited that field. Like many things in life, I tried to obtain control of my marriage as if it were a project. It's the only way I knew how to feel like I was achieving, and the only way I felt a sense that I belonged in the world. Before we married and throughout my relationship with my ex-husband, I experienced so much confusion. In hindsight, I think that he would have been an amazing best friend. But I pursued the marital relationship, because I believe it was an opportunity for me to change things in him and to change things in me. Emptiness, loneliness, lack of drive, were common feelings.

Soon, I had become pregnant and remained pregnant for precisely one week. During that week, I felt at my highest. I had found a purpose in my life, which was that of giving birth, or so I thought to myself. Little did I know that it was the start of a self-discovery journey. I felt like my ex-husband treated me with such care, attention, and love. And it t was one of the few times I had treated *myself* with kindness and nurture. Then, I had a miscarriage. And, as often happens after this type of loss, within less than a year, the marriage was over.

I now realize that, for years, I had not been available. I thought that I was, but in reality, I was an open wound. Soon after that relationship, I continued attracting partners that were not available. Either physically or emotionally, I now know that I was the reason for that attraction. (In this book, you'll also learn about that connection with your inner child.) These men were not available to me, because I was never available. From an early age, I trained myself to please, to achieve, and continue moving forward. I didn't notice that I was going through the motions without ever considering what I myself wanted from life, including formulating my own opinion, how I would spend my time, or what my hobbies were. At that time, I knew more about the expectations of the world outside than I did about myself.

Getting the Hint

At work, I attended a leadership course designed to help its participants improve their public speaking skills, and we were tasked with speaking about any general topic. Earlier that month, I had discovered a website (www.43things.com) where people posted anything important to them, including dreams, family, money targets, relationships, or finding "the one". I decided to speak about my experience using the website. I remember logging basic things that I wanted to accomplish, like traveling, saving more money, getting a promotion. As I was reading through other posts, one of them caught my eye. It was a prayer. One person posted content about how they'd been praying. I then started thinking that the last time I felt happy or in tune with myself was as a child, when I would pray. Something told me to post a prayer as one of my desires. I also added to that list to stop lying.

During the leadership speech class, I spoke about this experience in front of my colleagues. It was the first time that I had shared anything personal about myself at work. There is something magical and potent when one acknowledges real dreams, desires, wounds, and shares them with the world. It was the first time I experienced healing through a personal acknowledgment. It was also the first time that I had publicly shared not only personal information about myself, but also that I felt like I did a great job in any speech class. From this experience, I learned that speaking your truth is magic. Secondly, I learned that a chance to bring change to a circumstance starts an intent or decision.

The same relationship with my ex-husband that had brought me to work at a hospital helped me build not only the best of my relationships, career successes, knowledge, self-awareness, but also brought me to the purest love of my life. Without that marriage, I would never have moved to the place in the city that connected me to that job, that training. At this point, I started believing that things happen for a reason. And that sometimes, when you think you're losing control, you are genuinely entirely in control. But for things to manifest according to a larger purpose in the world, one must trust that process. To make a connection between what most would call a failed marriage and a success story requires a journey of "non-sense". But since I've started praying, life has been more giving, responsive, and enabling then in the seven years prior.

Better Times Will Come

After getting divorced and working through a series of unwanted relationships, I felt the need to enjoy life for what it is. I started attracting friends who saw the light that I couldn't see in myself. I started going out for myself and started being interested in activities like painting, writing, reading, and cycling. One extraordinary friend even introduced me to snowboarding. Never in a million years would I have envisioned myself on the top of a mountain, holding on to my life on a snowboard. During this self-discovery process, I also met a personal coach who saw the potential in me enough for her to take me on as her client. I would meet with her every week for an hour, or talk over the phone to discuss things that were bothering me.

For example, she described one relationship we discussed as "emotionally toxic", where the other person was not available. But I felt the urgent dependability and need, feeling like I had no other choice in life. I loved from a place of a wound. Through these torturous sessions in my coaching experience, I demonstrated to myself how wounded I must have been not to see the value of my time and my life, and that participating in a situation or relationship that was not serving me would impact many other areas of my life. It was then that I truly started to have an appreciation for coaching. I also thought to myself that, one day, I would become a coach. Throughout my life, I experienced and still experience big and small life challenges. Those things will not change. But my perspective, where I see value, and the way that I respond to those life circumstances differed tremendously. Regardless of one's circumstances, one thing hold true: change is constant, and our highest point in life is when we truly understand ourselves for who we are, speak our truth, and are disciplined enough to do the things that are right for ourselves.

Coaching also taught me prioritization and self-care. Relationships and aspects of my life that didn't serve me well eventually started removing themselves on their own. I was promoted four times during a seven-year working period. By the age of thirty-one, I was an executive at one of the most innovative health systems in New York, and probably the youngest at the time, leading critical programs that would facilitate cutting-edge programs to patients with chronic conditions. It was a dream come true. Still to this day, hearing the stories of the impact of our work, it's something that keeps me working in the field.

But I've become comfortable enough to know that the time has come to shift and transition to the next phase of my life. I know there's so much more to me. I've been procrastinating on the topic of coaching, primarily because there was fear, hesitation to put my own life out there. Writing this book, though, is healing in itself for me. The fact that I can impact and help others around the world, through my own experience, tools, and lessons learned is probably one of the most rewarding and fulfilling experiences I can ever imagine. So, recently, I've decided to shift my career to focus on promoting healthcare transformation across the country, using my voice and leadership to transmit inspiration and love. Specifically, empowering communities and people through my coaching practice. There are many reasons (or excuses, depending on how you look at it!) that I can share about why this is not the right time to write this book or to entertain the idea of having my own business. But, like everything else that has happened in my life, it has a purpose, and it carries weight in a bigger plan.

The Big Chop

One of the things that I wanted to do before I was able to plunge in was to continue my self-identity discovery path. One of the most significant endeavors was what the curly-haired community would call a transition. Three years ago, along with some of my friends, I decided to stop straightening my hair and leave it to its natural look and feel. Regardless of your gender, with straight or curly hair, with hair or not, you can appreciate the connection to perceived external beauty. One of several physical features that I questioned in myself, in addition to my weight, skin complexion, and overall persona, was the way that my hair looked.

At the age of nine, my mom started chemically processing my hair to straighten it. A common thing to do if your child had "kinky" hair was to apply chemical treatment. For about twenty-two years, that's what I've been trying to do, along with other damaging behavior such as high heat, or anything it would take to make it look straight. I think this move is also for the benefit of my readers to continue working toward the true self, because that's what I advocate. So, three years ago, I decided to cut my hair or, as they call it, go for the "big chop," removing all chemically processed hair from my head, probably the most difficult self-discovering process I have undertaken as an adult. I share this story, because part of your career transformation will involve removing relationships, values, beliefs, and other things that no longer serve you.

I cried and cried for almost a month. The result did not look right from my perspective. "I no longer look pretty," I said to myself. But then again, when was I ever comfortable with the way I looked? (It's limiting to see and respect yourself and others if you don't appreciate your original design.) So I would always be surprised when someone gave me a compliment.. Cutting my hair represented removing all the things that no longer served me away from my life. Seeing my hair short and curly, unlike what I've seen for the last twenty-two years, felt demoralizing to me. But since then,

I felt I have gone through a 360-degree transformation. Today, I *feel* beautiful. Not only have I gained a greater appreciation for who I was designed to be, but it has helped me see the beauty in others. Through this journey, I was criticized by many, including my mother, who has voiced how unattractive I looked. One may think, "It's just hair, so what's the big deal?" But for me, it reflected a part of me who's most meaningful desire was to meet external expectations. To please. Now, I wouldn't trade my hair for the world. It has been given to me as part of my design, and not embracing it would be rejecting who I am.

Aging Is Real

One would think a transition involves some form of a spiritual awakening or physical shift like a move or change in job, or an emotional shakeup such as a marriage or divorce, but they come in all different shapes. As I mentioned, another significant transition has been seeing my parents evolve and age. As I start nesting, I'm finding myself sandwiched between taking care of parents and my growing family. Growing up, I have always been closer to my dad. He was the patient, charming, comfortable-to-get-along-with parent, not to mention that he was and always will be so much fun. In recent years, though, his health has been compromised; he has developed Lewy body, which is a form of dementia. He quickly transitioned from being the life of the party to often staring up at the sky, not remembering the day of the week or the room he's in at a given time. In this way, I felt like I have experienced the death of a parent.

Although both he and my mother are alive, I often feel like I've lost my original dad. Regardless of your circumstances, the world has ways of reminding you, that one must experience every opportunity you have as things are. As I sat next to my dad at the clinic today, he lovingly held my hand and looked at me. He expressed how pretty my hair looks. This is the magic. These are the moments, when you know that the parent that once let you drive on top of his lap when you were six years old, is still there by your side. He is worth every minute of my time. I don't think there is ever enough time or space to prepare for caring for any loved one with any serious condition, whether that's Lewy body, cancer, or any other chronic concern. Your response to such events becomes critical. Regardless of whether you are in healthcare or not, the experience of a loved one having a disease is nerve-wracking. There is an emotional and physical re-prioritization of relationships that takes place when yourself or loved one goes through a health-related experience. Not only do you become very conscious of caring for your health and others, but you start realizing how fragile life might be. I look at my parents, and I see a history of hypertension, diabetes, mental illness, and cancer. And I ask myself how I can prevent all of this. Unlike my parents, I work in healthcare, and I have resources that perhaps weren't accessible to them at a younger age. What can I do differently for myself and others? I now strive to be the enabler of information and action for myself and others. Using an experience or lesson to change the course of your path and your community is growth in itself.

That's My Story

The primary reason why people are unsure about taking a leap of faith concerning any life event or transition, I have found, is that it is not an easy process unless it is organized and doesn't feel overwhelming. I could find ten excuses or reasons in one minute for why I should not be writing this book. It's probably the same ten reasons why you're stuck in the role that perhaps underutilizes you, feels like busywork, or you're ready for a change. By sharing my story, I intend to offer my readers a fundamental understanding of where I come from; also, I hope that giving you some context will demonstrate that I'm not superior or inferior to you, although we are different. The most meaningful lesson of all is that I'm no more or less extraordinary than others. Wanting to belong or "being somebody" was not my intention; that would be a reflection of my limitation. Aligning my thoughts, actions, and words with that of my core values was a requirement for me to live to my real purpose, including my career.

I've been blessed through my career journey, not because I'm extraordinary, as I thought one must be, but because of the amazing mentors, coaches, and resources, and a support system that have enabled me to reach the next level of potential. However, I attracted all of it only when I was emotionally and physically ready for them. It is essential to recognize that each one of us is born into specific families and neighborhoods, and throughout our life journey, we encounter day-to-day circumstances that often redefine us. But we do, however, have the ability to change and maximize those circumstances. This book will help you transition to the next step in your job or career, one that makes sense to you at the time, meeting you exactly where you are, regardless of your hair type! Grab pen and paper and a journal, connect with your heart, and body, and be ready to embrace yourself.

Chapter 3:
The SmartRise System –
Starting Your Career and Life
Transformation Journey

*"People are working harder than ever, but because
they lack clarity and vision, they aren't getting very far.
They, in essence, are pushing a rope with
all of their might."*
— Stephen R. Covey (*The 8th Habit:
From Effectiveness to Greatness,* 2004)

This chapter will introduce you to The SmartRise Career Transformation System. You are who you are, and steps to successfully set a career path must be aligned with your purpose, current life demands, and future goals, through a plan you will formulate throughout the book.

Why SmartRise? If you're reading this book, the odds are you are considering making either a job or career change. Perhaps you are losing interest in your current position, or you may be looking for a promotion or a change in role at your organization. Maybe you are on a journey of exploring what it is that you want to do with your life, or you're seeking a job that better utilizes your talents. You may have recently been laid off, or you're looking for more flexible hours, maybe more money. Or a place where your colleagues and management have a greater appreciation for whatever it is that you do. Perhaps you're looking for a better work-life balance. There could be multiple reasons why you grabbed this book. Regardless, you need a plan that will help you find clarity on what it is that you should be doing and an approach on how to get you there.

As a life and career coach, I have noticed it's usually not just about making the change in your career. It goes beyond just finding a new job, updating your resume, going to networking events, and applying to a new job. To effectively find the right career path for you, we first need to find an ideal job for you. For us to get you there, I'd like to welcome you to dig deeper into your authentic self. The common challenge most people encounter, including myself, is that if you don't know where you are, you can't determine what your next step will be. Career change is a natural life progression; it becomes a person's ever-evolving path toward achieving material means, but also freedom and purpose. A smart process and person looks within first, to understand the resources and barriers she has to plan for the next steps.

Let me introduce you to The SmartRise system. The term comes from the notion of using the person as the source of tools for determining the next steps and development, and from there, have them rise to their fullest potential. The system promotes and looks into critical aspects of a person's life journey to inform career course and priorities, while building a path forward and transitioning to their new role. The system includes guidance, lessons, and techniques that can help you transition down your path with ease.

One of the main reasons why most change systems fail is because most people are looking for a replica process of what has worked for others. You see, that's the first and foremost mistake. Each person has a path and position in this world that's perfectly designed for them. It's crucial not only that you understand it, but embrace and have a plan so that it's foolproof. If you follow it, it works. If not, it will not work – it's that simple.

The system looks at the following areas of your life as you build a career plan that works for you. It starts with sharing tools and assessments that help you understand that you are your most significant and most valuable asset. Seeing and appreciating your talents and gifts will help you gain insights on your strong suits that you'll carry throughout your life. Additionally, you will be better positioned to sell them to your next prospect or client. We will also take a look at how these areas interact with your personal balance. In parallel, the book will be providing you with tools to achieve maximum results in critical areas of your life. Ultimately, you want to have the best perspective and personal position so that you can be as effective as possible in your new shiny career. Let's look at these steps in order:

Step 1 - Career planning

You will understand and learn how to use your talents and gifts to embark on a purposeful career path as you transition to a new job.

Step 2 - Making it happen

You will learn the importance of prioritization and action planning. Prioritizing and action planning will increase your productivity at your job by channeling your energy in the right areas and avoid feeling overworked, busy, and underutilized.

Step 3 - Personal growth and self-management

You will learn and embrace that the evolution of your growth is key to finding the job that's exactly right for you.

Step 4 – Financial prosperity

You will learn to identify your financial intent, set SMART goals, and how to use your career to achieve financial success.

Step 5 – Inner and spiritual connection

You will learn to design your career journey with purpose, action, and balance by tapping into your inner resources as a source of guidance and wisdom.

Step 6 – Relationships

You will learn the power of relationships, how it influences your career path, and how together we achieve a larger purpose.

Step 7 – Contribution and Community

You will understand how giving and sharing your talents and gifts increases the flow of abundance and fulfillment into your career and wealth.

Step 8 – Health and Wellness

You will learn how to read and nourish your body in order to support a transition into a new job and to feel confident with job security.

Step 9 – Physical environment

You will learn how to organize your physical space to maximize your creativity and productivity as you continue to advance in your career.

Step 10 – Fun and Recreation

You will understand how doing more of what you love builds up the physical and mental capacity necessary to strengthen your motivation and performance at work.

The [Real] Reason for Career Change

It's vital that throughout the book, you make a note of the rationale and purpose behind your desire for a career change. As you assess the different areas of your life, the driving force behind the change may become more visible. Why is this important? Because the origin will inform what's the best approach and path is appropriate for you. This becomes key as you continue to uncover your career desires, and are steps closer to your new job.

Setting Your Career Goals

Setting career goals is a critical piece to The SmartRise system. We will be using SMART goals that will help you stick to your plan and track your steps and successes. SMART is an acronym for Specific, Measurable, Achievable, Relevant, and Time-bound. Your goals will be achievable and trackable, which will encourage you to continue following your journey as you quickly see results. Each chapter will review critical lessons and techniques that will prepare you to draft your SMART statements that make sense to you.

Knowing What You Want

You may not know precisely what you want at this time. Or you may have a clear idea of where you want to go. Regardless of your current state, this book will keep you focus on the necessary steps to identify what your "thing" is, as well how to get it.

Fundamentals of Bringing Change and Abundance

You have the power to bring abundance into your life. Too often, I see people chasing happiness and successes. Much of it they already have; it's a matter of tapping into the source and knowing there's more to it than meeting specific goals. The SmartRise system is based on the principles of gratitude, dreaming and thinking from a place of endless possibilities, not fear or limitation. Always start with thanksgiving; be thankful for what you already have and see the miracles that come from this one simple act.

Identifying Yourself – Your Talents and Gifts

Your decisions lead to your destiny. Do you believe that? You should. It's true. Sooner or later, what you do – and who you are – determines what you ultimately achieve. The beautiful thing about your talents and gifts is that they can build upon themselves. If you can get the snowball rolling, the energy of motion will take over. Think for a moment about the people you respect. Why do you admire them? You are probably drawn to them because they are full of realized potential. When we see people exerting this kind of energy, it compels us to bring ourselves closer to them and become a part of what they are doing.

Opportunities and success are not something you go after necessarily, but something you attract by becoming an attractive person. Continued development of your skills and refinement of all the parts of your persona will attract the right career path or job. The opportunity will probably seek you out. So today, you have a choice. Will you sit at the top of the hill merely contemplating your capabilities? Or will you give yourself a little shove and barrel down that hill, knocking over obstacles standing in your way?

Career as Part of Your Life

Remember: Your job is part of a much larger path – your life. How you use yourself as a resource, prioritize your efforts, and use other areas of your life determines your career path. Focusing exclusively on achieving career goals without addressing or balancing other areas becomes a trap, one that continually brings you back to a feeling of limited fulfillment and a lack of purpose. Without a meaningful, useful and actionable plan, you will continually seek the next steps, or feel stagnant, with no escape from your current reality.

Your Resources

The SmartRise system uses yourself as its main asset, and then it builds up from there. It starts by identifying your core values and assets and then leverage other areas of your life to make you stronger and more authentic in being yourself. You, as a resource, are the most critical asset. The book will introduce you to resources that will help you align and balance all life component. Including maintaining your health and tapping into your inner strength to align your career path with your life's purpose.

Developing and Mastering Your Career Plan

Growing and learning within your plan requires a change in mindset, to believe that your dreams indeed will come true. Everything begins in the heart and spirit. Think: every great achievement began in the spirit of one person. They dared to dream, to believe that it was possible. Allow yourself to ask, *"What if?"* Think big. Don't let negative thinking discourage you. You want to be a "dreamer." Dream of the possibilities for yourself, your family, and others. If you had an idea that you let grow cold, re-ignite the desire! Fan the flames. Life is too short to let it go.

Exploring the unique, endless possibilities within you, then, will become your mission. Remember that when you work on improving yourself, you're adding to the youth, vitality, and beauty of your mind.

Exercise: Now, start by writing yourself a thank you letter to yourself for embarking on this fantastic journey for yourself, while being grateful for the beautiful next steps you will construct and accomplish.

Chapter 4:
You – Your Most Important Asset

"You and your purpose in life are the same thing.
Your purpose is to be you."
– George Alexiou

Over the course of your life, you will ponder on the thought of caring for your belongings, having the latest phone or car, saving money, and accumulating wealth. Ultimately, one thing is constant. For better or worse, you are stuck with yourself for a lifetime. Perhaps you had very little control over what family you were born into or the body and brain that was given to you, but from there on, it's all on you. For example, you have free will to retain and change skills. Investing in yourself and your growth will become the most meaningful activity as explore your career growth. Therefore, we must learn to care for our bodies, mind, and spirit, and to absorb information the way we're each individually designed to effectively function. The first step in doing so is centering yourself. Then you'll be positioned to explore your values and strengths, and to prioritize your time and fully embrace your authentic self.

Quiet Your Mind and Fuel Yourself

One of my biggest life challenges has been the battle between being conscious of today. Often referred to as "the now." There's substance and appreciation for one's value when we're aware of the passing moments in life. As I write this passage, I'm on my way to Austin with my husband. We just tied the knot. It's been quite a journey, coming from past fears to the place I am in today. Before that journey, today would have been a very different day. A typical day for me would have been obsessing over what I need to do at work next week. Or what my bank account should look like in ten years, or the meaning of life. Those thoughts come and go, and they have a place and time. When I start obsessing, I quiet those thoughts down, and instead I grab and kiss my husband's arm.

You see, it's a balance between two things. First, planning for the future is critical toward achieving one's dreams. Second, the past contains lessons and experiences that can guide us. But the present is unique. We're unable to replicate it because, as soon as it happens, it disappears. Whether it is significant and memorable, like the day of my wedding, or practical, like sitting on a plane. You have assets, and blessings are available at all times. This is important to recognize, because it brings a level of gratefulness that keeps you actively grounded on the now.

Maybe it's just me, but as we get older, it feels like times go very quickly. One day my husband and I were talking about why that is. My conclusion is that our schedules are so cluttered with work, social, and life matters that we're consistently paying attention to the next thing, always on the go, connected to notifications at all times. Rarely is life quiet and in silence. But silence is indeed needed. I fuel through silence.

Exercise: Describe the ways you fuel or re-fuel. Think. Is it through quiet time? With friends? Social gatherings? Both? What is it that you can't wait to do after a day at the office?

Exercising your natural fueling state allows for an easy progression of the best version of yourself and for extending its shelf life. The goal is to fuel in the way that works for you. Your days might feel longer, for all the right reasons. Spending your time absorbing the moments throughout the day becomes the way you get closer to your internal GPS, the one that guides you, gives you options … we often call it gut feeling or intuition.

Exercise: Think of your life for a moment and breathe in. Close your eyes and imagine yourself in a happy state. What does that look like? Where are you? Are you by yourself, with someone or others? What are you doing? Write it down. Do this for seven consecutive days, then review what you've written. If you forget, start again on day one. This exercise will help you put the pieces of your life puzzle together. It will confirm feelings, or further along your understanding of your path.

During my moments of silence, I become steps closer to what my life purpose is at any given time. By that, I mean that I'm getting to know myself just a little bit better. Throughout my life, I learned to accommodate others' wants and needs very well. Everyone's but my own. I said "yes" to most things others needed from me. As I've shared, I created the most sophisticated mask of all: the mask of a "pleaser". It was celebrated and appreciated by the other person, but it wasn't necessarily getting me closer to meeting my purpose. Instead, even further, it's hard to take the masks off once they are on. They take years to remove. Unfortunately, many go to their graves with them on, never allowing themselves to celebrate their purpose. Let's not be one of them.

Exercise: How do you know if and how many masks you're wearing? Well, take a look at the purpose you decide to work every day. Are you empowered and confident? Right in place and creative? Are you concerned and empty? How do you feel about going into work? Are you excited or pooped? Do you act differently at work, at home, with friends, with your significant other?

Living in the moment is important, but living in the moment combined with authenticity takes it to whole new level. Not only will you experience longevity, but those times when authenticity shines, it exponentially adds substance to your value, your being, and your legacy.

Understanding Your Values

Appreciation of yourself, comes with an understanding of what matters to you most and the areas where you have the most impact to yourself and others. Especially as you rethink what's next in your career and your life, identifying values becomes a way of prioritizing your time, interactions, and opportunities. There are several lists out there that will help you understand the values you consider most important to you, and we'll review some of them in this book.

It's critical to note that there is a difference between your natural and "acquired values", those that society, our family, co-workers, or friends may think are important, and thus, they have become essential to you. Or it's possible that a value is dependent on another value, making it an "acquired" or "secondary" value. Here, I'd like you to focus on primary goals. These are money/happy-makers. I've provided a list of values to consider. Values perceived by others may be different from your values. Ideally, your values and those recognized by others around you align or are the same. Alignment is an indicator that your inner and outer world are well connected, and that you manifest the energy you carry within.

Exercise: Select your top five to ten values that speak to you, that you live by, the reasons and motivators you get up in the morning. You can identify your values by using any of these approaches:

- Think of experiences or circumstances that you felt empowered, excited, bursting with energy, and you felt good about yourself. What value do you think was heightened?
- On the flip side, think of a moment that made you feel uncomfortable, frustrated, or angry? What was bothering you, and what value do you think was being compromised?
- Deal-breakers: What values are show-stoppers for you? After breathing and having a pulse and food, what's next? What do you need in your life? Otherwise, the world feels pale. Is it creativity, calmness, stability, purpose?

Examples of Values

Acceptance
Accomplishment
Accountability
Accuracy
Achievement
Adaptability
Alertness
Altruism
Ambition
Amusement
Assertiveness
Attentive
Awareness
Balance
Beauty
Boldness
Bravery
Brilliance
Calm
Candor
Capable
Careful
Certainty
Challenge
Charity
Expressive

Cleanliness
Clear
Clever
Comfort
Commitment
Common sense
Communication
Community
Compassion
Competence
Concentration
Confidence
Connection
Consciousness
Consistency
Contentment
Contribution
Control
Conviction
Cooperation
Courage
Courtesy
Creation
Creativity
Credibility
Health

Curiosity
Decisive
Decisiveness
Dedication
Dependability
Determination
Development
Devotion
Dignity
Discipline
Discovery
Drive
Effectiveness
Efficiency
Empathy
Empower
Endurance
Energy
Enjoyment
Enthusiasm
Equality
Ethical
Excellence
Experience
Exploration
Liberty

Examples of Values

Fairness	Honesty	Logic
Family	Honor	Love
Famous	Hope	Loyalty
Fearless	Humility	Mastery
Feelings	Imagination	Maturity
Ferocious	Improvement	Meaning
Fidelity	Independence	Moderation
Focus	Individuality	Motivation
Foresight	Innovation	Openness
Fortitude	Inquisitive	Optimism
Freedom	Insightful	Order
Friendship	Inspiring	Organization
Fun	Integrity	Originality
Generosity	Intelligence	Passion
Genius	Intensity	Patience
Giving	Intuitive	Peace
Goodness	Irreverent	Performance
Grace	Joy	Persistence
Gratitude	Justice	Playfulness
Greatness	Kindness	Poise
Growth	Knowledge	Potential
Happiness	Lawful	Power
Hard work	Leadership	Present
Harmony	Learning	Productivity
Professionalism	Significance	Thorough
Prosperity	Silence	Thoughtful

Examples of Values

Purpose	Simplicity	Timeliness
Quality	Sincerity	Tolerance
Realistic	Skill	Toughness
Reason	Skillfulness	Traditional
Recognition	Smart	Tranquility
Recreation	Solitude	Transparency
Reflective	Spirit	Trust
Respect	Spirituality	Trustworthy
Responsibility	Spontaneous	Truth
Restraint	Stability	Understanding
Results-oriented	Status	Uniqueness
Reverence	Stewardship	Unity
Rigor	Strength	Valor
Risk	Structure	Victory
Satisfaction	Success	Vigor
Security	Support	Vision
Self-reliance	Surprise	Vitality
Selfless	Sustainability	Wealth
Sensitivity	Talent	Welcoming
Serenity	Teamwork	Winning
Service	Temperance	Wisdom
Sharing	Thankful	Wonder

Adapted from Leadershape (2020), https://www.leadershape.org/

Once you made your selections, bucket them into the following 12 categories: Integrity, Spirituality, Achievement, Intelligence, Feelings, Freedom, Strength, Courage, Creativity, Order, Enjoyment, Healthy Presence. Categorizing values will help you identify themes and see if there's any dominant value. Alternatively, you can use the Core Values Index (See Appendix) tool. (Note: This is a free tool, with options to receive more advanced reports for a fee.)

Knowing Your Core Values Shifts Your Behavior to Authenticity

Once you have awareness, some things are simply non-negotiable. You may want more awareness because those values bring fulfillment. Or, you might start avoiding specific environments, routines, and behaviors that no longer serve you. Throughout one's lifetime, your values remain pretty consistent, although your approach may differ. The more authentic you become, the more in touch you are with your core values. For example, I lead with achievement, with freedom, love, and wisdom. In my core values index, I identify as the Innovator-Merchant, which indicates that I thrive in environments that foster learning, knowledge sharing, and wisdom. There's a presence of loving knowledge when I walk in the room.

The beauty of this is that we each carry a presence with us when we walk into the room, sometimes fogged by other factors, like stress or misaligned priorities. But our existence is beautiful and needed at any place and time. That's why it is so essential to understand your presence, so that you can practice and embrace it. In a job or career, this comes into play quite often. How many times have you felt that you're underused in your job? Or perhaps it is no longer the place for you, but you may not be sure why? You say to yourself that it's too much work, too much politics, or that it doesn't bring you the passion it once did.

Exercise: Create two written lists, of twenty values that matter most to you and of twenty values that matter least. Set aside the two lists for one day. Come back to the two lists; review what words you have listed and see if you have any changes. Select the top ten values that you have listed for each of the two lists in order of importance. You have now cut the two lists in half. Review your ten values for both the list of what matters most and what matters least. Select the five values from each of the two lists that you feel are the most important. You now have five core values that are most important in your life and five values that you think are least important in your life.

Over the next several weeks, refer to these values as you assume your daily activities. Are you living a life that supports your core values, or have you found you are following a lifestyle that is out of alignment? Being out of alignment from your core values is a source of stress that causes many people to be unhappy and un-fulfilled. A personal check-in with your core values, as needed, is a great way to get back in synch with who you are and where you want to be headed.

Exercise: Now, the next step is to rank your core values and determine if you are giving them enough attention. Assess how well you're honoring each of the five core values by scoring each one on a scale of 1 to 10, where ten represents optimally living the value.

What's your level of satisfaction with each value?

Be honest with yourself and assess areas that are not meeting your expectations and fullest potential. Add an action step to each one that indicates the process or something you'll do to increase the score in that area. If it's important to you, spend time enjoying each one. Don't feel like this is yet another task to add to your list. Instead, if these indeed are your core values, it should feel good about them.

You now have your core values and ranking. Next, you'll want to understand how to use these values to make decisions. These mainly come in handy during transition periods, such as in career planning and transformation. We can use the process to map out your career plan and future actions. Imagine yourself doing more of what matters to you more of the time.

Exercise: Close your eyes and visualize. Where are you? Describe the setting, whether you are sitting or standing. What are you doing? Who's with you? Imagine each of your values being in an enhanced state. For instance, if you chose health and wellness, imagine yourself having more energy. You play with the kids and run with the dog, and you come back home feeling invigorated. You have chores to do, but hey, life is good. Whether exercising your values on day-to-day activities or deciding you want to become a nurse, you can prioritize your natural tendencies and preferences, your way of being. This initiates a self-asserting behavior that first considers yourself as the source of value, and of value towards a greater path beyond just a career or job.

Strengths, Gaps, and Opportunities

As a unique individual, you possess particular strengths and weaknesses, your attributes, while your values are what matter most to *you*. Founder of positive psychology Martin Seligman outlines two characteristics of what he calls strengths:

1. A strength is a trait, a psychological feature that can be seen across different situations and over time.
2. A strength is valued in its own right. The strengths are states we desire that require no further justification.

This second characteristic also highlights another essential difference between gratifications and pleasures; unlike pleasures, gratifications are undertaken for their own sake, not for any other positive emotion they may produce.

In his ground-breaking work, Seligman offers twenty-four different strengths that are measurable and acquirable:

- Creativity
- Curiosity
- Judgment/Critical Thinking
- Love of Learning
- Perspective
- Bravery/Valor
- Perseverance
- Honesty/Integrity
- Zest
- Love
- Kindness
- Social & Emotional Intelligence
- Teamwork
- Fairness
- Leadership
- Forgiveness
- Humility
- Prudence
- Self-Regulation/Self-Control

- Appreciate for Beauty & Excellence
- Gratitude
- Hope/Optimism
- Humor/Playfulness
- Spirituality/Faith

Reviewing the above list, do certain strengths stand out in your mind?

Discover Your Personal Strengths

How can you to discover your natural strengths? Here are two options:

1. Register for a free account on the University of Pennsylvania Authentic Happiness website (See Appendix) and take the VIA Survey of Character Strengths.
2. The VIA Institute on Character (See Appendix) offers the survey on its website as well.

(Note: These are not the same tests. The VIA Institute assessment has half as many questions and takes ten to fifteen minutes to complete. The University of Pennsylvania assessment takes closer to twenty-five minutes to finish.) They are both scientifically research-validated and they have shown improvements in the following areas:

- Improve your relationships
- Enhance your overall wellbeing
- Build your resilience
- Strengthen your ability to overcome problems

These are critical areas that one must attend to under any circumstance, especially when planning for career or job change – before, during, and after.

Play to Your Signature Strengths

Seligman suggests that each of us has a set of core strengths, what he calls *signature strengths*. As presented earlier, your signature strengths are *the top five strengths* from their survey.

Discovering your natural strengths can be an instructive process. It may clarify what you already know about yourself or highlight strengths you aren't conscious of.

For example, let's say your top five strengths include: honesty/integrity, creativity, humor/playfulness, teamwork and love of learning. You may benefit from having a career or job where the organization has a culture of learning and fostering employee experience. You're in a position of designing or developing solutions without compromising your integrity, and employees are in a collaborative space of ongoing dynamic interaction. You may not perform at your highest in a structured traditional hierarchy setting. Discovering your natural strengths helps inform how to make the best of your time and in what conditions or settings you're likely at your highest performance or state of growing and perseverance.

Although we may aspire to possess a high proficiency in all twenty-four strengths to master every valued human virtue, the reality of our human identity provides a more realistic view.

Capitalize on Your Signature Strengths

How does Seligman suggest you increase your level of authentic happiness? Use your signature strengths every day in the main areas of your work and life.

Exercise: Once you know your top five strengths, take each strength and ask the following:

- Where am I using this strength now in my work?
- What are three to five ways I can use this strength more consciously in my work?

Next, you can answer the same questions about your home life. The more effort you invest in developing skills in your strength areas, the more gratification you will experience in the present.

Circle of Concern and Circle of Influence

Stephen Covey's classic *7 Habits of Highly Effective People* is probably one of the best reads out there, and as the title implies, it focuses on how to establish structure in your daily routine to ultimately became effective. Covey starts his book by determining what's first things first – yourself as the most important asset, emphasizing the importance of focusing time into one's personal mission and identifying the roles that you take on in life and prioritizing each of them. The second piece that will help anyone seeking a career path and having influence through your actions is the Circle of Concern and Circle of Influence. A Circle of Concern encompasses the full range of concerns we have, such as our health, our children, problems at work, the amount of government borrowing, or the threat of war. A Circle of Influence encompasses those concerns that we can do something about. They are concerns that we have some control over.

Stephen Covey defines proactive as "being responsible for our own lives ... our behavior is a function of our decisions, not our conditions. Proactive people focus on issues within their circle of influence. They work on things they can do something about. The nature of their energy in doing this is positive, enlarging and magnifying. They increase their Circle of Influence. Proactive people focus on issues within their circle of influence. They work on things they can do something about. The nature of their energy in doing this is positive, enlarging, and magnifying. They increase their Circle of Influence. Reactive people tend to neglect those issues that are under their control and influence. Their focus is elsewhere, and their Circle of Influence shrinks."(Covey, 1989, digital version).

A useful way of determining which Circle you are in is by listening to the language used. This can be applied to yourself or within a group, regarding work or any life aspect, for instance, career, personal growth and relationships You can distinguish between the use of the words "have" and "be." Circles of Concern are full of "have's," while Circles of Influence are full of "be's." The table below provides some examples.

Have's (Reactive)	Be's (Proactive)
I'll be happy when I have a full establishment...	I can be a better role model...
If only I had a boss who wasn't...	I can be more organised / resourceful...
If I had respect from...	I can be more loving / understanding...
If I could just have management days...	I will be more diligent...
If the environment was more conducive...	I can seek out personnel and be able to understand...

From Covey (1989), *7 Habits of Highly Effective People.*

As you can see, the <u>Circle of Influence</u> (See Appendix) takes your concerns and narrows them down to areas of impact, which, more often than not, makes the change from external to internal. From hoping things and circumstances would be different, to emphasizing what you can do differently to address the concern. Isn't it great? Keep this in your forever toolkit. I've used it time and time again, because each day, sh*t happens, and you need to continue moving forward. Some days are more severe than others, but regardless of your circumstances, the table above can be applied. The goal is to keep you accountable and focus on your areas of priority, without having you running short on fuel.

For example, my dad was diagnosed with cancer and Lewy body dementia about a year apart from each other. I remember being away on vacation, coming back to the devastating news. I would categorize this issue as serious when compared to other concerns I had at the moment. I still do, but my initial response was more reactive than proactive: if only he just had more support to help him make the doctor appointments; if only he had a different lifestyle maybe this could have been prevented; if only doctors would just give him better options – you know the ones we all want to hear – no side effects, high survival, and good quality of life. A cure would be excellent.

It's no surprise a serious health condition is probably one of the worse things we can experience, but even so, there's a circle of influence in everything. My more proactive approach to the same situation includes sharing my father's scheduled appointments with other family members, understanding that his life choices and health, although very important to me, are not mine. I can educate him on how to eat healthier, exercise more, and access support groups. Whether he follows my advice is a separate matter.

From my perspective, I have increased my influence, by listening more, being more empathetic. I still have a long way to go, because as we all do, I lose patience. Also, communicating with the doctors involves my dad, mom, and sister as much as possible, so that any decision making is done as a family unit. This can be applied to work, too, during high-stress seasons. If you have my type of job, it's high stress every day, and I use this tool as my sanity keeper.

Exercise: Select your top concern and write down the things you're doing to address them. Don't overthink this. I want you to use the terms that feel natural to you. Are you more reactive than proactive or vice versa? Write down the things that are within the Circle of Influence. Regardless of the concern or how you're addressing it, there's an inside and outside the Circle of Influence. If you find that there's an item that you cannot resolve within the Circle of Influence, then the action is to let it go.

"If you don't behave as you believe, you will end by believing as you behave."
– Fulton J. Sheen

Essentialism

As we learned, we're all very different and are driven by our core values. I struggle with focusing on one task. I feel like an octopus; I enjoy many hobbies, and have several strengths that can apply to several areas. So how do you focus? You have to pay bills and need to make a living, right? Well, an eye-opener for me was reading Greg McKeown's *Essentialism*. It is a must-read for bringing focus into what's important not only for your job but all areas of your life. Over and over again, I see people switching careers in hopes that the next task is not as overwhelming or that they're not spread too thin. What you don't want to happen is that you switch jobs and careers, and you bring old behavior that leads to the same feeling in a new setting. As we've learned from Covey, the Circle of Influence keeps our focus on the areas where we genuinely have an impact. McKeown takes it to another level in providing strategies for how to stay in that Circle, and the value it adds as assets to achieve your goals.

McKeown's model is based on the fundamental importance of gaining control over one's actions, and those that specifically that have high value/return, which yields doing less while building capacity for what's important. The Essentialism model reflects the following:

McKeown's Essentialism Model

	Nonessentialist	Essentialist
	All things to all people.	Less but better.
	"I have to"	"I Choose to"
Thinks	"It's all important."	"Only a few things really matter."
	"How can I fit it all in?"	"What are the trade-offs?"

table continues on next page

McKeown's Essentialism Model

	Nonessentialist	Essentialist
Does	**The undisciplined pursuit of more**	**The disciplined pursuit of less**
	Reacts to what's pressing.	Pauses to discern what really matters.
	Say "yes" to people without really thinking.	Say "no" to everything except the essential..
	Tries to force execution at the last moment.	Removes obstacles to make execution easy.
Gets	**Lives a life that does not satisfy.**	**Lives a life that really matters.**
	Takes on too much, and work suffers.	Chooses carefully in order to do great work.
	Feels out of control.	Feels in control.
	Is unsure whether the right things got done.	Gets the right things done.
	Feels overwhelmed and exhausted.	Experiences joy in the journey.

From McKeown (2011), *Essentialism*, pg. 8

So if you wonder how you're going to fit this career plan into your world for the next several days, months and years, this approach is a key to your career plan, and also ensures that you're successful and fulfilled in any career path you choose. For instance, about seven years ago, I was asked to work on a "mission impossible" project (i.e. unrealistic deadline, barely anyone who would even understand the tasks and milestones needed to be accomplished, lack of resources to do the work), but it brought a great sense of accomplishment to work for it for six straight weeks while going to bed at 1 a.m.

That was the same time when I would typically reassure anyone that my main priority was my family and health. Clearly, that wasn't the case.

In *Essentialism*, McKeown nicely explains the power of saying "no" more often, and how others value you more when you first recognize yourself as a valuable and almost rare asset. The book taught me to check my intent before undertaking not only major projects, but in any basic positioning. As I've shared with you, I fuel from achievement, and as a child, I was often rewarded with "good jobs" when I achieved these critical, barely possible projects. As adults, we no longer get medals, trophies, or even thank you's sometimes, so being able to see my efforts bring a conclusion to a major organizational project was wonderful. However, there are several ways I could have accomplished the same objective, without putting my health at risk or even working so many hours, and still be viewed as a key contributor.

For example, when someone asks me to join a meeting on my day off, for instance, my natural response before reading this book was, "Of course I'll be there." Why was that my natural response? Because it felt good to be needed. I received appreciation through feeling needed. Is this a good reason to join the meeting? No. Fast-forward to present, the same question is still asked. My answer is "*No.*" What changed? I'm truly living to my priorities. I took a day off to take care of my health, or an errand, and so I consciously made the choice to not be at work that day.

In this section, you might learn that who you are is one thing, and the way you act is another. Throughout our lifetimes, many of us, including myself, have sworn that the most crucial aspect in their lives is family or their spirituality, but in reality, when you take a closer look, where you're spending your time and where you're pouring your love reflects something else. Don't worry; it happens to all of us. We all change, and it's important to reassess our priorities throughout our lives. Our priorities shift for many reasons, and it usually starts with a transition.

Transitions include any significant life events that may alter one's physical or emotional state. This may consist of marriage, loss of a loved one, divorce, new job, moving, having children, etc. Makes sense, right? If you're like me, they happen in threes. Crazy, but it doesn't fail, and my skin gets angry (which is also typical for me). So we must take the time to realign our wheels before we add another event or refocus our attention.

Exercise: Life Balance/Balance Wheel: Ranking and Assessing Impact

The "Wheel of Life" (See Appendix) exercise helps us look at the various life functions which we address daily. It is not unusual to find ourselves pulled in one direction or another and ending up focusing most of our attention in only a few areas of our lives. When this happens, other areas of our lives get neglected. As we learned through McKeown's *Essentialism*, setting priorities help us advance in areas that are truly meaningful to us.

This exercise is designed to help you determine whether you are focusing too much on one part of your life and, consequently, neglecting others. The graph depiction of a wheel can be segmented into six sections. These categories may vary depending on the individual, but with these categories as a template, consider how much of your time do you spend in each of these areas over a week:

- Career and Finances – your employment path and income
- Significant Other, Friends and Family – quality time spent with friends & family
- Spiritual and Personal Growth – your spiritual connection
- Physical Health and Wellness – taking care of your physical body
- Physical Environment – life at home and in the community
- Fun and Recreation – your leisure time activities

Assign a number from one to ten for each category. The number "one", depicted as closest to the center of the wheel, represents the least amount of time, and the number "ten", furthest from the center, represents the greatest amount of time. Plot a dot for this assigned number on the corresponding concentric line in each area. When you connect the dots for each category, you will see how balanced your life is. Next, looking at the six categories, list them in order of satisfaction in your life. Next to each group, indicate how much time per day you spend in that area. The purpose of this activity is to identify how you currently spend your time on the major demands of your life.

Satisfaction and Time Spent in Each Category

Satisfaction level	Time spent per day
1. Career and Finances =	
2. Friends and Family =	
3. Spiritual and Personal Growth =	
4. Physical Health and Wellness =	
5. Physical Environment =	
6. Fun and Recreation =	

If your wheel of life is very uneven, it may reflect the current demands placed upon you. A large, well-balanced wheel can reflect a happy, successful, and satisfying life. But a balanced, satisfying life does not mean that you spend the same amount of time in each area. Some areas will need more attention than others depending on various situations that come up. And one source of stress is ignoring your core values based on shifting external demands. So let's delve into the meaning of your responses.

Look at your satisfaction scores. What are the two lowest scores?

How much time per day do you spend on each of these categories? What can you change to improve these satisfaction scores? What would be the ideal level of time to spend in each of these areas so that you could be more satisfied?

Review your satisfaction scores. What two are the highest scores?

How much time per day do you spend on each of these categories? Is there anything you need to change in these categories?

After you have reviewed your findings, return to your Wheel of Life graph and, in a new color or perhaps a dotted line, plot what you would consider to be *ideal* amounts of time in each of the six areas. You will notice a gap of time in certain categories. These are the areas of your life that need attention. In some areas, you may be spending too much time, and in other areas, you may be spending too little time. Perhaps it indicates that you may be placing others' needs ahead of your own. Again, this exercise visually depicts how you currently spend your time. As you review the six areas of the Wheel of Life chart, consider your neglected areas and identify what things you could start doing to attend to these areas. Consider what activities are taking you away from your focus and priorities. How can you change this?

Also, this exercise is an excellent starting point for establishing goals. Well defined goals – SMART goals – help you to create a target destination and help you create a clear action plan to regain this newly aligned sense of balance in your life. The positive result of completing this exercise is that you can reduce stress and live a more rewarding experience, while you simplify your life.

As I mentioned, categories can vary from person to person. Using slightly different categories, the Institute for Community offers a colorful depiction of the wheel. Matching your use of time with your current life priorities allows you to avoid the sense of overwhelm that can have adverse effects on your health. Learn about yourself by completing this exercise. Who knows, you may discover new strengths and abilities you didn't realize you had, and this could lead to a great way of sharing your talents with others. Life's journey includes finding your life balance and fulfillment.

Once the wheel exercise is complete, look again at the segments and gaps, and review using the questions below:

- Does this surprise you?
- Which areas are higher than you thought?
- Which areas are lower than you thought?
- Does this line up with what you value?
- Which areas are most important to you?
- How can you make changes to improve those areas?
- What changes can you make in the next three months in two of those areas?
- Who can you share your commitment with?

The Big Why

Now that you have figured out where your real priorities fall, let's refocus our attention on why you're reading this book. Why are you making the change: money and salary, change in jobs, appreciation and recognition, layoff, stress, flexible work options, career opportunities and advancement, looking to change careers?

Similar to the wheel of life, looking at why you're seeking a change, will help us see the opportunities moving forward. Write five things that come to mind when you ask yourself, "Why do I want to make a change?" Do you feel like you have no other choice? What would you lose if you don't make this change? If you had a magic wand, forgot obligations and barriers, and you had limitless possibilities, what would you do? Make a note of your responses; we'll refer to them again.

"You were born a child of light's wonderful secret –
you return to the beauty you have
always been."
– Aberjhani, *Visions of A Skylark Dressed in Black*

Numerology

One of the beautiful fascinations of the universe that I have been surprisingly connected with is numbers. Numbers speak to me, better than humans sometimes. But we each have a thing that speaks to us, and the more you practice being silent and getting to know yourself better, eventually, you'll identify what that thing is. How do you know when you've found "your thing"? Well, for me, I see the number three often, in clocks and license plates, when I need a confirmation. Call it coincidence, or the law of attraction, regardless of what it is, sometimes the universe speaks to us by making something resonate with meaning for you.

Speaking in the language of numerology, one of the most common ways of discovering the roles of numbers in your life is by identifying your Life Path number. The Life Path (See Appendix) number is a key to understanding your life's purpose, innate tendencies and talents, and the obstacles you'll face as you continue to master the lessons to be learned. The Life Path number indicates the primary mission in life – it outlines what you're learning, mastering, and evolving into. So while you will have innate gifts and talents in this particular arena, you might also have more distinct or heightened obstacles in getting there.

My life path number is seven. Based on the details of that path, it is no surprise to those closest to me that I'm independent, that I ground and invigorate from being by myself. But without socializing, or not trusting in myself or others, I close out and shut down. As much as I love being around my friends and family, I've learned to recognize the line. The same happens when I participate in large speaking engagements, and I feel completely wiped out.

On the other hand, activities like hiking, swimming, and biking feed me (which reminds me, I need to do more of these!). It doesn't mean I like one more than the other. But in understanding my source of battery life, I enable myself to focus and balance throughout the week, so no particular area falls short. Of course, this is only the way it works for me, for my life path.

Get to know yourself through the perspective of numbers. Take note of any exciting findings or keywords that are closely aligned with who you feel you are.

Exercise: Identify a tangible or intangible object or symbol that you'd like to use as the method the universe speaks to you. Something you are drawn to. When you have a question, need guidance or reassurance, use it. Communicate with or focus on it, trusting that the answer will lead you closer to your need. What's your life path number? What does it say about your natural tendencies and personality?

Making Space

Let's talk a bit about making the space to think about all the things I've asked you to journal so far. Creating space for the items you want in life is the true meaning of priority. I'll walk you through an example using one of my favorite series, Comedy Central's *Broad City*, Season 5, Episode 4. For those not familiar with the series, it was filmed in New York City, focusing on the shenanigans of two women in their late twenties to early thirties (by the end of the final season). Most of the content is fun and mindless entertainment, and some way, somehow, this episode truly hit home for me. Ilana discovers that her roommate Jaime is a hoarder and shortly after sets up a candlelit atmosphere and plays a therapist, encouraging Jaime to open up about his problem and feelings. She is using a pizza box as her writing pad, like a real therapist. In this way, Ilana created the space for Jaime to feel comfortable sharing his fears and concerns.

On the other hand, Abbi tries to make the jump from the sweater folder to window artist at a local Anthropologie store as an attempt to making her footprint and space for her art. Unfortunately, it resulted in her getting fired. Not cool. Although, we may see this as a failure, it started Abbi's self-discovery journey. She started making the space, by taking a leap of faith, one that released her from what seemed like a safe space (i.e. steady income), to one of uncertainty, forcing her to rethink her purpose and artistic talents. Bottom line: The concept of space is super, super important. You need to make space in the sense of time, but also area in a physical state to set the goals and know where you're most grounded.

Exercise: Refer to your focus areas identified during the wheel of life exercise, and answer the following:

- Do you make sufficient space for it?
- Do you have a room in your home or a place outside, beach, gym, park, store, that fuels you?
- When do you feel most like yourself? Who are you with?

These questions will help guide you to areas where you need to make the space, whether it is physical or an allocation of time.

The big life maker for me in the last year has been gratitude. Wow! Making space is the action, but the driving force is gratitude. Being appreciative for the things we have in life is something we're often taught as a child. *The Magic* by Rhonda Byrne is a beautiful read for those seeking a way to change perspective. I highly recommend it during your transformational journey. The idea that you'll be entering another transition, filled with barriers that you may or may not see, and being grateful for the things that have not yet occurred, was probably the most important knowledge I've gained from this book.

How can you be thankful for what's not here, however? Thanking myself for paying my credit card bills or sending myself a check to the future Vanessa, seemed a bit "out there" initially, until I started seeing the present and future results. This action also opens our eyes to see the many things we take for granted each day, like plumbing and functional cars. I no longer whine about my car not turning on when it has a bad day; it's functional most of the time, and that matters. Practicing gratitude will open the doors to meeting the right people in the right place in the right circumstances for your career to fully flourish. Not only will it help you be more attractive to the right offers and opportunities that work well for you, but more importantly, you will feel good about it; and gratefulness positions you to be a magnet for success and the spread of your authenticity.

Exercise: It's important to concentrate our attention using visualization to help with clarity and focus. Create a vision board, using collages, text, pictures; the images should illustrate what you envisioned yourself in the next several months, maybe years. As you gather each piece, thank each one for its contribution to the version of yourself you are creating. Keep the <u>vision board</u> (See Appendix) accessible or visible throughout the day.

The Right Tune

> *"Judgment is a negative frequency."*
> – Stephen Richards

I often get folks expressing how tired they feel each day, going through the mundane day-to-day tasks that fatigue them and do not inspire them to explore or to do anything differently. If that is true for you, keep your judgment in check. You start believing and living your thoughts, so perspective and attitude are vehicles of your life commuting. You have the power to change your approach and view of each day. (As I write this passage, I have a long week ahead of me, between work travel, writing this book, and family commitments, not to mention the things that for sure will come up by the end of the day that will be added to my to-do list. I can be a miserable, take it out on my loved ones – more often closest to us, since it's much easier to take them for granted casually, and it's easy to play victim of my actions. Yes, I've chosen to do all these things and join you in a transition, as I'm going out and entering another. My choice.)

The first step in changing attitude is to be accountable for your actions. Second, focus on your Circle of Influence we discussed earlier. It's much easier than to try to change others and circumstances that are simply out of our control. Each person is responsible for his or her own path. You hear this often, and I will repeat it. By bettering yourself, you're able to give more of yourself to others.

Exercise: Write down recurring thoughts in your mind for the last week. Has there been a theme? If so, is it usually about work, relationships, a special event, your finances? Are there thoughts of concern, person, or story you've been replaying recently? In one sentence, describe the emotion you feel when you're thinking about it.

The purpose of this exercise is to do an emotional frequency check. The frequency check gives you a current view of where you're directing your emotions, thoughts, and, therefore, actions. Consciously choose your outlook on what you do, what you can, and what you will. Choose to find joy in chores. They have to get done anyway, so you might as well do them in light and gratitude. This may feel like settling to some, but there's a balance. It sets you to respond to each day proactively, and to be grateful regardless of circumstances life throws at you. It also sets up a strong foundation to handle barriers or excuses, depending on the perspective that you may encounter as you evolve your career, life priorities, and attitude. Remember: You become a magnet for the things you release to the outer world. Choose to attract opportunities, the perfect break, the right circumstances for you.

"Our way of thinking creates good or bad outcomes."
– Stephen Richards

Planning and Discipline

You now have several tools and assessments that provide you with a better understanding of your natural inclinations. You also understand that without seeing your value ... well, others certainly can't. Understanding what we value is crucial as we develop our careers. You know what makes horrible salespeople? Not believing in their product. And you can only go so far, hoping others see your potential, when you are not convinced.

Planning and discipline are the next steps, as we assemble all our learnings to create a reasonable plan that you can stick to daily. Throughout the book, we will be using SMART goals to keep you on track and honest with your goals.

1. **Specific** – Aim for a particular, concrete area for your goal or steps. For example, "make ten job search calls following up on my LinkedIn connections" versus "make some networking connections."

2. **Measurable** – To determine if your goal is measurable, ask questions such as: how much? How many? How will I know when it is accomplished?

3. **Attainable** – Goals are most attainable when steps are thought out clearly and allow enough time. How do you intend to accomplish your goal? Which actions follow on other efforts? Is the goal realistic given where you're starting from? It should be a challenge, but also achievable.

4. **Relevant** – A relevant goal is one that matters to you and the result. Is it worthwhile? Is this the right time? Does your goal relate to other efforts

or timelines? Does it require resources that are currently available?

5. **Timely** - A goal should be grounded within a defined period, both for clarity and to give your action urgency. When do you want to begin? When do you want to complete each step?

Tips to achieve your goals include:

- Write down the steps. Write down your goal and the steps to get there. This will help you remember and complete each step. Post your list where you will see it often.
- Set deadlines. Give yourself a date to complete your goals. Write the date when you actually will finish each step.
- Reward yourself. Taking steps toward goals is hard work. Think of small rewards to give yourself when you complete any step, to help you stay motivated.
- Have a goal partner. Find someone to help you stick to your plan: a friend, co-worker, a job coach, or someone else. Discuss your goals and check-in with them when you complete the steps. If possible, do the same for your partner!

Here are some examples of SMART goals:

- I will get adequate sleep every night starting next Monday, by going to bed at 9 p.m. every night. I'll put all the electronics down by 8 p.m. As a reward, I will stay up until 11 p.m. on Friday nights. I'll talk to my wife so we can do this together and keep ourselves accountable!

- I will wake up 30 minutes earlier each morning to write ten things I'm grateful for, starting this Saturday. I'll set my alarm forty minutes earlier than usual to make sure I'm up on time. As a reward for sticking to my plan for 21 days, I'm going to reward myself by getting an excellent massage. I'll text a person I'm thankful for each day to keep me on track, plus brighten someone's day!

Now, for each item described below, develop a SMART goal. Take a look at your life wheel assessment results and for each area identify if there's something you can do differently, frequently, or no longer do. For example:

- What can you do differently to take care of yourself?
- How can you increase your practice of gratitude?
- What can you do differently to change your perspective and attitude?
- What changes can you make to gravitate towards your natural tendencies and or avoid your pitfalls?
- What can you do differently to address your concerns better? Refer to the Circles of Concern and Influence.

Understanding what matters most to you kicks off the process of informing your next steps, about how and where to spend time, and your priorities. Taking into consideration areas of your life that may need extra attention, your natural strengths and self-exploration will emphasize the notion of self-value and worth, which is an important and fundamental step in your career plan. As you start designing your career plan, pay attention to the learnings from this chapter. Then any business or job should fit your natural progression.

Chapter 5:
Step 1 – Start Your Career Plan

*"It is not what to do, but how much love
we put into the doing. We can do not greats,
only small things with great love."*
– Mother Teresa

In this chapter, you will understand and learn how to use your talents and gifts to embark on a purposeful career path as you transition to a new job.

Don't Overthink

We often get caught up in overthinking what we need to do and often almost obsess on the barriers. We lose sight of what, in reality, is essential to us. I'm big on pouring love into all the things I do. I'm often asked, "How do you do so much?" My default answer, "It's beyond me, it's bigger than me. It's love." Call it God, inner spirit, your source. It's clear to me that the magic comes from love. Only love and fear exist; then, all other feelings follow. I choose to love, and the universe finds a way to respond using the same language.

For years, until recently, I found myself knowing that something else is out there, but not necessarily being unhappy, just feeling kind of stuck. It's the worst feeling.

Knowing something is off, but not entirely putting your finger on it. "What is it?", you might ask. Well, for me, this is usually the sign of a transition period. It's a phase in which your body, mind, and soul are adjusting for the next stage. This may happen every couple of months or several years apart. For me, it's clear when I'm in it. The world seems foggy, almost like everything is in slow motion. I'm fatigued and forgetful. It's almost as though a magnetic field is consuming every particle of my body, and what remains is purely for purposes of survival, to breathe and have a pulse each morning.

My last run lasted several months, and it was brutal. But, man, did I have power coming out of that thing! So for months at a time, I've been waking up, but not having a purpose. For me, that's a big deal, since as you've learned, I feed off completion and achievement. I would go through meditation, prayer, and connection with my inner source for guidance, and one day, it all came together. I combined a series of techniques that involved all parts of my life in finding what I needed to focus on.

My passion has remained in healthcare, but more recently, my heart has led me to community work. Many will hear that for the first time, through this book, and wonder, "What's next for Vanessa?" Well, I'm uncovering each part of it and enjoying each moment. That's the beauty: when you come out of a transition, you see each step and past events very clearly, and make the connection as of why things are happening the way they are. Why does this matter? Because for you to effectively move forward with your career path, you must trust the process. Don't mess with the process. The moment you interfere, the universe will not be as effective at performing what is best at: inspiring action. It's a common phrase, but it's a real deal. Things that come naturally are the best.

Coming from a person who spent countless hours doing things forcefully to please everyone but myself at a younger age, I've since learned that once you trust and act on behalf of yourself as the greatest asset of all, everything comes together naturally. When you try to take control, in many instances, you may not realize that you're trying to obtain power, but things start falling apart again. So why do we care so much about doing things our way, having control, but not enough of us act on our behalf to make the change we want to be and see? Because it's in our brains to do the same things we did the day before. Not going to bore anyone with the neuroscience behind this, but it's real. Each day we aim to seek purpose, because it's our natural pull. It's our inherent value, and your mission is to be you.

"I just want to do something that matters.
Or be something that matters. I just want to matter."
– John Green

Using Personality Traits and Core Values to Plan Your Career

Success comes from using your natural inclinations, often called talents and gifts. This chapter focuses on how to get a better understanding of what these are so that you can focus on enhancing them as you evolve in your career path and know how to use them. We briefly learned about personality traits in the earlier chapter to help identify the appropriate path as you transition to a new job. A strong plan is flexible and adaptable to life changes. More importantly, it is one that's not connected with a feeling of "happiness". Plans are just a series of steps, and flexibility allows for detours. Our ability to welcome changes and circumstances as lessons makes our plan or outcomes that much more amazing.

Let's start by circling back to what's important to you. In the previous chapter, we referred to these as your core values. Your core values will bring light to your key motivators and tendencies. Now that we know your strengths and core values, we want to push them out there. As you make use of them, you will also learn your shortcomings, and you will be in a position to address them by approaching them using your core values. Full circle! You address challenges and barriers, using your natural strengths and core values. Wonderful. You are now positioned to conquer change and all of what it will bring.

Exercise: Let's map your career now. Creating a career map or plan for the future doesn't mean making a ten-year plan. Instead, it's about taking small, actionable steps every day and bringing the right attitude and behavior forward. Consistency will become a unique tool that you will use to drive change. Structure does not take away the adventure, creativity, pleasure, or spontaneity from life. Instead, it builds space for it. The mundane, and things that no longer serve you will have a position in the universe; they simply no longer fall on your shoulders.

Having a pathway toward your ideal job is the simplest and most effective way of achieving business and career goals. Not having a clear vision will lead to quickly losing sight of what's important to you and comforting yourself in the virtues of familiarity. We've all fallen into that trap.

Note: No two people will likely have the same career plan. Answer the following questions. Some of the items you may answer from the previous exercises. When answering, come from a place of abundance, and don't forget your magic wand; if you could do anything, even multiple things, what are they? Don't place any limitations, like time, age, education or training, title, etc. Your answers should reflect only an abundance of possibilities that we will then make practical later. The goal is to work this process in parallel as you continue developing or transitioning to the next phase of your career. It's okay if you do not know the answers; sometimes trying a new role or training will identify the answer to these questions and place you closer to your ideal job. Got it?

Career Planning Questions

Exercise: Answer the following questions, from a place of abundance:

1. Why do you want to transition to another job or career?
2. What does transition mean? Different organization same job function, promotion but the same organization, change in organization and job function, or change in industry or job type, that is, financial analyst to a dental hygienist? Entrepreneur to full-time job with organization or vice versa?

3. What do you have to lose if you don't make this change?
4. What, specifically, do you want to do?
5. What have you done before?
6. What are you good at?
7. What do you like to do?
8. What is your current/desired career path level? Select one that applies:

Entry-level: Recent graduates of high school, undergraduate, or graduate and professional programs. If employed, titles might be trainee, associate, assistant, etc. This group typically is still exploring and encouraged to try different job functions to develop their strengths but also to understand their core values better.

Mid-level: People who have been promoted from an organization's entry-level. This role typically involves oversight of and responsibility for direct reports. Standard titles are "manager," "supervisor," "associate director," etc. This group will probably have had experience or recently started learning the need or value of coaching direct reports. They often are jammed in the middle of front level staff needs and leadership expectations. This group also tends to experience the highest level of transition, such as marriage, children, health, or other priorities.

Executive: Common titles include "director," "vice president," "partner," "principal," "managing director," etc. This group usually has worked up to have the level of autonomy other groups are working towards. These are typically your organization's strategy, financial, and operational decision-makers or as relevant to the industry.

Encore level: Typically, a person who is approaching retirement age (fifty-five years or older), regardless of station or level. He or she might be seeking to stay active and competitive in the workforce, or maybe looking to move out of a traditional role and into another area of interest or passion, either compensated or as a volunteer.

Detour: Person is challenged by having been without a job market due to a layoff, downsizing, or a personal need, such as child-rearing or an illness. He or she could be returning from a sabbatical, from running a family business, or from military service that took him or her off course. This person might be starting a business after having held a more traditional job, or maybe looking for a traditional job after having been self-employed for some time.

The next step is to identify what actions to undertake depending on your path level and progression timeline. For each question, create SMART goals to describe how you're going to achieve each target.

At this stage, you're probably wondering, "How am I going to do this?" You have the tools. You know what you're good at. Great. Even if you don't, the reality is that you're one step closer to pursuing or making the change you've been waiting for.

You may be tempted to now put the book down to rest and run! The remaining chapters will help you align the rest of the areas we identified in your wheel of life so that this process is as smooth as possible. For each area, you will come out with concrete steps that put you closer to a job you love! All are tying back to your career objectives.

The biggest mistake I see time, after time, is that people say, "If I get promoted, I'll be happy. When I get an increase, I'll be able to afford all the vacations I need." As you'll learn in later chapters, the pursuit of happiness is trivial. Instead, purpose and intent that originate from many areas of your life will bring you the fulfillment that means something to you. Feelings connected to an action or goal may result in short-term fulfillment. Instead, growth that comes from within, matched with external needs, results in long-term career success.

Job Fulfillment

As you prepare your plan, here are some useful tips on how to gather your ideas and develop your how-are-you-going-to-get-there SMART goals.

One stumbling block can be being too job-specific when considering a possible career. Once we do this, we can get easily discouraged and limited in our thinking. Think about the field of work rather than specifics – for example, if you love helping and being around animals, then a veterinarian job may be an idea, but there are lots of other options, such as becoming a professional dog walker. The idea is to think outside the box – skills for one job may suit another kind of job – like a teacher's skill at explaining convoluted topics and using language well to convey the message may make a good writer.

Research the Possible Qualifications Needed

You may have a list of possibilities, so now it's time to research what you would need to know or what qualifications you may need to achieve your dream job. Perhaps you're considering setting up your own business, so looking into business classes could help, or maybe you need to go back to school and get a degree. Find the different steps you need to take and don't feel deterred.

Get to Know People in That Field

Exercise: To begin, consider networking. Ask around your friends and family to see if they know anyone in a similar field you could chat with. Find online forums or groups that discuss the area of work of interest. By talking to others, you will get more of a feel of the work and even advice on how to get started.

Evaluate Your Findings

Once you've done some research, make sure you take stock and evaluate what you've found out. Does this career fit in with the lifestyle you want? Consider the information you've gathered and work through the pros and cons. Does it still excite you? Do you feel passionate about it? Will it involve compromise you're willing to take, or is it too much compromise? It's always important to check in with yourself.

Sign Up for Experience and Training

A good option is to look around for volunteering opportunities or internships to get experience or see if it's really for you. You have nothing to lose. Instead, you're gaining more insight into what you do and don't want to pursue. It can also eliminate any unneeded areas of study or training elsewhere, or help you understand what skills you do need to develop.

Once you're positive and excited about your new career adventure, then signing up for gaining the necessary qualifications is the next step. Remember to keep focusing on each step, to prevent feeling overwhelmed or anxious.

Keep a Positive Mindset and Don't Give Up

Our mind is powerful and can determine whether we give up or succeed. Keeping on your path requires a positive mindset. It's going to feel daunting and a great leap of faith to change your career, but by believing and following your passions, inspirations, and happiness, you will allow yourself to realize your potential to be happy in your work life. Don't let others deter you with their limited thinking or opinions. Just keep on your path, with your ultimate happiness in mind, and see where it takes you.

By now you have a good understanding of core values, strengths, and the perspectives you must create in order to design and sustain a successful career plan. Think of your learning up to this point as the foundation to your career house. Appreciating yourself as the greatest resource towards personal and career growth is the base. Understanding your values and natural inclinations are the columns and beams that keep you steady. Your behavior, mindset and perspective allow for your personal growth overtime. The next chapter will guide you on how to stick to and execute your plan. Get ready for the ride!

Chapter 6: Step 2 – Making It Happen: Prioritizing and Sticking to Your Plan

"If you don't like something, change it. If you can't change it, change your attitude."
– Maya Angelou

This chapter will focus on the importance of prioritization and action planning to help you to stick to your career plan, and to increase your productivity at your job by channeling energy in the right areas and avoiding feeling overworked, busy, and underutilized.

For years, I had gone with the flow, either through networking or recommendations, without really thinking through my natural strengths or the things I wanted to achieve by the time I was thirty. In some cases, I consider myself blessed to have put the puzzle pieces together. There's an intrinsic power to trusting that you will be in the right place at the right time. When that happens, you want to be ready.

I must say, I had great mentors along my career path, and people who identified and saw me as an essential asset to their organization, but it definitely helped that I was always in search of the things I was really good at, and that whenever there was an opportunity to work outside of my role or immediate title, I went for it. Assessments are a starting point, but what closes the deal is acting on your desires and plan. Throughout my career journey, it's been an even exchange of hard work and my network pulling me up to the next level.

You may still be stuck debating between what career or occupations may apply or be relevant to you based on your strengths, core values, and where you are at in your career path. If this is the case, then follow the next steps:

- Explore different types of occupations.
- Interview people in professions that sound interesting to you.
- Based on the results of your self-assessment and research, what careers seem like a good match?
- Identify your preparedness for these careers.

What's the difference between career planning, plan, and roadmap? Do you need all of them? Yes. Each one will help you get more specific about what and how you will accomplish your career goals. Is it worth it? Yes. Your information will be so granular that finding a job will become seamless.

Career planning conducts a gap analysis, looking at the distance between your wants and the current situation and how to accomplish your goal. A roadmap provides a picture of how you will achieve your goals by collecting all the information from your assessments and learnings in one place. A plan then tells you with specificity and using SMART goals to ensure you get to the holy grail of an ideal job. But let's not be fools. The key to a successful plan is to aim but let go of expectations of the journey. Your plan is a guide in line with your vision and direction. Life brings barriers, challenges and surprises that may change your course. You will learn to use your wisdom to understand the best way to respond to each circumstance that will then inform your next steps. To make things happen, two actions are required. First, you must drop the past, both successes and failures. Second, you decide that this plan will work. Doing so, makes space and kicks-off for the work of today and the outcomes for tomorrow, and the journey in between.

If you recall from the last chapter, we touched on the topic of using your core values to make decisions. McKeown's model imbeds a great deal of making a conscious choice or making decisions that perhaps you're not accustomed to. If you're like me, I really have to pause and think to say no, even today. I check my intent, that is, why should I say yes or no? The *real* reason. What's the tradeoff? Usually the tradeoff involves things that matter in my life. Career is very important to me, but other things are, too. Take a look at your core values, and use them to evaluate your tradeoffs and risks, whenever you are placed in a position to prioritize.

Also, refer to your wheel of life assessment results; those values with the lowest points are usually the things that "give" when we prioritize other things. Saying no, doing less, does not pose career risks. It's actually the opposite: by focusing on fewer things that add true value, you help the organization become more efficient and successful. Also, the odds are that you will not burn yourself out, feeling resentment and depleted of all joy for what you may enjoy doing. I've experienced both, and look back at past experiences knowing that there were things I could have done differently, but also trusting the timing. I'm grateful to now know and to pass this along.

We've discussed the importance of planning on and setting SMART goals. This next step is understanding the approach, your natural approach to implementing the plan with finesse.

Bringing It All Together

It is key that you use the fundamental concepts learned in previous chapters so that you're successful in completing your career plan. Here's a summary of your must-do's as we move forward.

- Make the decision to move forward with your plan.
- Trust that the plan will work, and that you have exactly what you need to find the job that you love.
- Know that dreaming and believing will open unlimited possibilities.
- Practice gratitude. If possible, read *The Magic*. If that book is not accessible at this time, at your library or to own, make a list of ten things you are grateful at the beginning of each day.
- Complete the suggested assessments before completing your plan. Know that, by completing the assessment, you will uncover untapped content about yourself that will set you up for several years to come.
- Find space and time visualize what your plan will look like when all is complete.
- Suggested reads (the resources mentioned earlier in the book), while not required, work very well in parallel with this book and kicking your plan into gear.

- Be consistent with your plan and own it. Plans that are taken seriously only when time allows do not work. Prioritize yourself and your time.
- Be open. Throughout the rest of the book, we will touch on key aspects of your life. It all works in sync, and not only will you have a complete plan, but you will be come out stronger knowing that you will be successful in the next phase of your career journey.
- So if you wonder how you're going to fit this career plan into your world for the next several days, months, and years, this is going to be a key to your career plan, but will also ensure you're successful and fulfilled in any career path you choose.
- An effective plan includes options for all contingencies. Even if you feel very sure now about what you want to do five years from now, things change. Having a Plan B and Plan C doesn't diminish your commitment to your plan A. Going through the process of creating your plans will help you learn about yourself and open a world of possibilities you may not have considered.

Self-Assessment

Exercise: The next questions will help you summarize your self-knowledge and confirm that your plan reflects the things that matter most to you, including your natural strengths and inclinations.

Knowledge, Skills, Abilities

- What are the three to five areas of general knowledge I have?

- What are the three to five areas of specialized knowledge I have?
- What are the three to five areas of specialized skills I have (compositions, statistics, language, etc.)?
- What are my top three natural abilities?

Interests

- When I have spare time, I like to …
- I wish I had more time to …

Values

- Identify your top five to ten most essential values. Write a brief sentence or two about why they are crucial. You bring them from your Chapter 4 assessments or add any others that connect for you.

Personal Characteristics

- List five characteristics that best describe you.
- List five characteristics that describe how you'd like to be.
- Ask three friends/family members how they would describe you.
- Ask three colleagues how they would describe you.

Identify Possible Careers

The following are a few resources you can explore to research careers:

Online:

- Occupational Information Network (See Appendix)
- Occupational Outlook Handbook (See Appendix)

- <u>GradSquare</u> (See Appendix)
- Your professional association
- <u>Linked In</u> (See Appendix)

In-Person:

- Informational Interviews
- Alumni networks (from both the university and your department)
- Your professional association

Based on your self-assessment:

- What careers interest you most? What makes them appealing?
- What careers make the best use of your assets? In what roles are they best used?
- List at least three job titles of interest to you.

Strategies for Entering your Chosen Profession

Exercise: Based on the results of your self-assessment and research, what careers seem like a good match? Evaluate your preparedness for these careers below.

Gap Analysis

- What do you still need to learn about your career choices?
- What do you need to do to be competitive for these jobs?
- What employers hire people in these positions?

Career Roadmap

Exercise: You've done a thorough self-assessment. Now, identify your preparedness for these careers.

- Review strategies for entering your chosen profession at a given level.
- Based on your gap analysis (see Gap Analysis Chart Key in this section), ask yourself, "What levels of these skills does my desired occupation require?"
- Which do you need to develop?
- What specific steps will you take to close this gap?
- What professional organizations are relevant?
- Continue to build your network in your desired field, around your desired job.

Exercise: Finally, prepare for your job hunt.

- Develop a branding statement. For example: A registered nurse connects with others in personal and unexpected ways to provide top-notch care to emergency room patients. Or, an elementary school teacher uses field trips and a little magic to inspire students and instill a love of science in children.
- Write a CV or resume.
- Write a generic cover letter.
- Identify the best job search resources for this field, noting where are posted.
- Practice interviewing with a friend or using online resources and videos.
- Similarly, learn about negotiating.

Gap Analysis Chart Key

Description	Performance level
No knowledge or experience	0
Basic knowledge/experience	1
Minimal knowledge/experience	2
Moderate knowledge	3
Highly skilled with extensive knowledge	4
Recognized as an expert	5

Chapter 7:
Step 3 – Embracing Your Personal Growth: Attracting Your Ideal Job

"To become more successful, you do not have to change who you are – you have to become more of who you are."
– Sally Hogshead

This chapter will show you how to focus on your evolving growth, centered around your personal qualities as a critical component to finding the job that's exactly right for you.

Sally Hogshead is a very talented woman that I truly admire and follow. In her book *How the World Sees You,* she describes the importance of understanding how others see you, not for confirmation or approvals (which is often what I've done), but so that your core values better align with what the world sees. When the inner world meets the outer world, it is like an explosion of fireworks, and it's exactly where we all want to be. No more masks, no more adjusting yourself to get your point or plan across. It becomes about how you communicate and natural expressions and connecting with others as you improve both your business and personal relationships.

Buy buying her book, you also receive a free personal profile, which allows you the opportunity to take a personality test and understand your two <u>Fascination Advantages</u> (See Appendix). I lead with *mystique,* with a secondary *power.* Together, I'm a methodological thinker; I may not be the life of the party and getting to know me takes time, but once there, people appreciate the value I offer. Communicating effectively once you understand your type is key, because it's not about how you get along with people or having the same views as the rest of the world. It's about how to embrace who you are and interacting with the rest of us in a way that offers strengths, effective marketing and engagement methods. Pursuing a career and attaining success requires exactly this.

After you've subscribed to her emails, Sally will send ongoing communications related to your personality types, effective marketing, and branding and communication tips. It may be time for me to take another assessment, since I've been through at least three major life events this year alone. As we've learned we evolve based on our experiences, current circumstances and insights into our future. My recommendation is that you perform assessments after a transition at a minimum, which most of us experience at least every one to two years.

Inner Bonding

You now have a better understanding of your inclinations, talents, and strengths. We're perfectly designed as who we need to be. Personal growth focuses on the evolving nature of opening and unpacking you. It does not translate a need to "improve" yourself. Improvement gives the impression that we're deficient, inferior, or superior. Instead, personal growth implies getting closer to your original and unique design. Think of downloading a software or application so that it installs, and the user can access all its functionality. In this case, you are both the download and the user. How great is that?!

Personal growth is not a ritual or something that you do once and are done. It's a lifetime of intentional effort to continue knowing more and using yourself to maximum capacity. Sometimes it involves a better understanding of concepts, but many times, it's about exposure to less familiar areas, so that we also get to learn more about others.

Self-management focuses on your ability to follow your thoughts, actions, and words, so that all are flowing from and manifest your inner persona, but also so that you can effectively respond to external information and influences. It includes discipline, connection with yourself, and core values.

What are the ways to work on personal growth and improvement of your self-management skills? Let's start by listening to your inner guidance. Inner guidance can be many things; some refer to it as a gut feeling, inner child, or spiritual guide. Whatever speaks to you, we need to tap into it.

Exercise: I first learned about the inner child shortly after my divorce, when I kept unfortunately consistently attracting people, not just for romantic purposes, that were not available. I then found Dr. Margaret Paul's and Dr. Erika Chopic's free

<u>7-day course on inner bonding</u> (See Appendix). It primarily focuses on the following:

- Healing anxiety, depression, addictions, and failed relationships by addressing the pervasive pattern of self-abandonment – shame, self-abandonment, shame – that is causing it.
- Healing the deepest fears and false beliefs that keep otherwise highly functioning individuals trapped in self-destructive patterns.
- Enabling individuals to make decisions that are truly right for them.
- Freeing up suppressed energy that is wasted on the destructive intent to control feelings, other people, and outcomes.
- Creating a connection with a personal source of higher love and wisdom, leading to inner peace

Throughout the week, you'll be exposed to the information you need for each day. They recommend you complete the assessment first, so that you have a baseline understanding of the root of the healing that needs to happen as you embark on this journey. Each day you will receive an email that explains and engages you on a self-dialogue with yourself. It brings you back to identifying your child or younger self, which is essentially your "original" design. Experiences, ideals, external influences are piled on, which created your wounds, whether it is addiction, insecurities, emotional obsession, attachment issues, etc. You want to speak to the original version of yourself to get to the root of things. We all have wounds, big and small, that are subject to interpretation. The first thing to do is not to judge. Otherwise, you are not objectively connecting with your inner wisdom and imposing your external view on your original self.

For example, one of the first exercises is learning how to have a dialogue with your inner child. Quickly, my little one (who's brilliant, by the way, and carries so much wisdom) felt like I would always prioritize someone else. It makes sense; I was taught to please and give to others first. I didn't know how to give it to myself. So I asked her, "What do you want from me?" She was clear: rest, nourishment, and not be too hard on her. Cut her some slack. As I write this, she's reminding me that I need to get better at this.

For many of us, this will not be a straightforward exercise. Especially if we were subject to emotional or physical trauma, the child itself is hard to reach. But regardless of the circumstances, it was not the child's fault, and without the connection, you will be unable to move forward past the psych wound that developed over time. To effectively attract the right job, people, and circumstances, this is a crucial step. Otherwise, you will continue feeling only temporary sensations of satisfaction at each phase and stage. Or you may attract something that sounds great conceptually, like more money or higher-level title, but will not connect deeply with where you intended to be at this part of your journey.

When you successfully find bonding between your now and inner child, you will move forward in life swiftly, and with compassion toward yourself and others. It's difficult to be hard on yourself when you have a mission to meet, like finding a new job because you dislike your current one, or looking for that next thing that excites you. Connect with your inner child as you would speak to a friend. Know that you're more than the body you see reflected in the mirror. Have dialogues when in doubt, when you need guidance on a specific situation, or just for fun!

As you practice inner bonding, over time, you will become integrated into one self. You'll remove any fatigue, anxiety, limitations, and emotional baggage. It will also help you shift to a different perspective. I promise you: your world will be different. Things that used to bother you will no longer be an imposition. People, maybe your friends today, may start automatically distancing. You may also attract new people that are better aligned to your path, and together enhance each other's personal growth. Random things will start happening, which is why it's important that throughout this journey, you release your control. You may say, well, that's easy or acknowledge that you're a control freak. Regardless of your situation, don't overthink and start asking questions, such as, "Why, all of a sudden, does this person not appeal to me?", or "How come I no longer like this drink or food?", or, "Why am I so sleepy?", or "Why do I keep waking up at 3 a.m.?" Let your body and inner guidance to decide what's best for you. Use your intellect for completing activities and logic to get you through the day. Do not resist or try to change any of these gradual changes; otherwise, you're compromising the process of healing. (You might be a lucky winner like me: I get hot flashes in the middle of the night.) Otherwise, let it go.

Take time to absorb your inner child before moving on to the next steps in this book.

Your Energy Profile

Now that we've connected with your inner child, the next step in the process is to take a pulse on your natural energy profile. Yes, we may see a body, arms, and torso, but our natural composition beyond the human state is energy. We're pure movement and particles that travel, bond, and repel. Cool, right? We all have different energy types, and because energy travels, we may attract and repel and carry things with us around. We also store energy for our survival, but also to be able to displace thoughts, emotions, and actions. All of our thoughts, feelings, and actions carry energy, which is why this is so powerful. Which is why there's such power in teamwork, aggregations, rallies, prayer groups, and meditation. When energy multiples, it promotes whatever vision it carries. (When you read or watch various news sources, you can quickly tell the energy the world moves on any given day.)

Have you ever walked into a room and gotten a weird impression, as though something tells you that you should probably leave? Or the opposite can be true as well, and it feels cozy and welcoming. We're describing energy. We'll talk about physical space and the movement of energy in your office and home at a later chapter. For now, we'll start by identifying your energy profile.

I learned about energy profile, when one day, I wasn't feeling the clothes I was wearing. If you're like me, you may have a closet filled with clothes, but you only wear your top five. Yes, this is common, and there's a reason for it. The energy profile teaches us about natural impulses and the unique ways we move around the world.

Think about your natural state and when you feel your best. Some of us have a faster pace than others. Some are bubblier or more serious than others. Have you ever found yourself doodling? I doodle triangles, love to fill in gaps and corners. My best friend doodles flowers and hearts. There's a reason for this (and some people can't doodle at all).

Carol Tuttle's energy profiling system is an incredible way of identifying the way to connect your natural being with how to feel your best. If you feel your best, you will act as well. You'll see improvements in relationships, your career, and just the way your true self interacts with the rest of the world. Take a look at the <u>Carol Tuttle's Energy Profile</u> (See Appendix) tool and see which speaks to you.

You may lead with one and have a secondary. (Do you want to guess what mine is, given some of the stories I've told? Ha!) But other profile characteristics come into play as well. This exercise is not boxing you into a category. Humans are complex and volatile in every way. We are a combination of all profiles, and one is not better than the other, so no judgment, please! But it's essential to have a starting point to work from so that you can be aware of your natural tendencies and where your energy is at its highest.

Carol's profile also includes an entire course of dressing your truth, where she provides tips (free and paid) services to help you "dress to impress." It's not only about looking sharp or put together. What's going to enhance your inner awesomeness is as essential. This is especially the case when you're interviewing or already in your new role. I also make it a point to boost my energy in the area of dressing when I'm feeling my lowest. It's easy to sit back and stay low-key when you're not as enthusiastic about your current situation. Instead, kick it up a notch and truly connect it to your inner persona. Everything should be in alignment. The way you think, to the way you look to the way you act. It's going to be a fantastic experience.

Exercise: So what are your next steps?:

1. Identify your Energy Type
2. Apply and embrace it to critical areas of your life, like family, love, money and career
3. Leap into your best life!

Have fun with this exercise, I know I truly enjoyed and laughed when it was so obvious what profile I was. I've applied to my friends and my now-husband, and it's so cool. You'll learn to appreciate each person for who they are, and stop trying to convince everyone intentionally or not to be like you. There's a sense of respect that I know you will earn from others as part of this exercise.

Akashic Records

We've explored your inner bonding your energy, so what's the next step? Well, I recently learned about is something called Akashic Records. We often use the phrase, "He or she doesn't understand where I'm coming from." Do *you* know where you're coming from? When you're getting to put words and concepts to the person you are, it becomes your mission to know more and more about you. Because it feels good to be yourself, once you find your natural rhythm and vibes, as one of my besties calls it. Imagine your doctor's medical records. They contain everything from your vaccines, medications, that weird rash you got last summer, your social drinking habits. Akashic Records contain everything, and I mean everything about you. Not in a physical space, but more about your energy's journey, including past lives, current life, and where you're going.

Akashic Records are not based on a psychic reading. It's an exercise that is performed so that you can better understand your path in a space that we don't see on a day-to-day basis. It's another tool to connect with your inner child guidance, love, or God, to obtain wisdom and guidance. To me, it has brought a sense of clarity on what I'm about and why my energy is the way it is, and why certain events needed to happen. When people receive information on the why, it brings closure and acceptance. I see this at work all the time. It solidifies that there is or was a higher plan that you understood at the moment.

I had my first experience with a very talented woman who provided me with insights that I needed to confirm regarding my career path, such as in what areas/industry is my energy used at its maximum. Her feedback aligned with the information that I already had handy from my assessments. For me, it translated to community work, charity, education, and children, which have been areas of interest of mine for such a long time. Although I contribute in these areas, it is not something I focused on as much as in other areas of my career. So for me, one of the next steps is to embrace more of that space, do it more with intention instead of just "when I have time," and tie it in with other areas of my wheel of life. I have embedded this into my career plan and priorities, and I am spending more of the time in these areas.

Akashic Records also give you insights on road-blocks that you may encounter in the future, given your energy and life history. Humans are pretty predictable when you have vital information. More so, this is the reason why history often repeats itself over and over, maybe just manifesting differently based on what's generationally relevant. But if wounds don't heal, acts of hatred and power struggles will continue to manifest throughout the world. If you wonder how to be part of the change, be the change. It starts with you and then overflows to others. Over time, I trust you will see a shift toward a place of love since all of us can position ourselves where it makes sense to each of us at any given moment in time.

Exercise: If you decide to try Akashic Records reading, prepare some questions ahead of your session. Here are some examples:

- What may I know that is in my highest good and best intention?
- How am I to serve?
- What may I know about my relationship to (person, family member, lover, stranger)?
- What may I do regarding (insert) (business plan, art project, difficult situation)?
- What may I know about a recent upset regarding (insert)?
- What stands in the way of my success?
- What may I know about the truth?
- Is there anything hidden or masked around (insert)?
- What may I know about healing an (illness/ sickness)?

Additionally, the practitioner may give you tips on how to tap your inner guide, so that at the comfort of your home, you're able to tune in and ask questions any day. This exercise was a tipping point in writing this book. I remember coming home and praying and meditating, while I asked for guidance on how I would get to the end of focusing on all those amazing things I know will fulfill me with joy. The creation of this book was undoubtedly one of the answers.

Core Values

As you continue down the path of understanding yourself, go back to the core values you have selected in previous chapters, and confirm/change as needed. Remember: Because there can be so much clutter with how to perceive ourselves and others, it's important that you identify any inaccuracies related to your initial impressions. If you change anything, keep a note of the changes, because it will help bring clarity as to why perhaps you made individual decisions in your life. It is essential to stay in constant connection with your core values, inner wisdom, and bring the truth out to others, as together, these will drive and influence your decision making.

Experiences and Learning Network

This chapter is all about learning, your insides, your outsides, even things that only your kiddie-self can tell you. Impressive. Let's tap into emotional awareness as a method of learning and further advancing the skill of using your emotions as an asset to absorb and respond to information. The term most commonly used is Emotional

Intelligence. According to Daniel Goleman, who is considered a pioneer in this area and whose books contain a wealth of knowledge, identifies five components to Emotional Intelligence (EI):

- Self-Awareness
- Self-Regulation
- Motivation
- Empathy
- Social Skills

Why does it matter? Emotional Intelligence is considered a soft skill, a less tangible skill that encourages a better understanding of non-verbal, behavioral cues to adopt, inspire others, and overall build interpersonal relationships. Whenever you see someone who seems to have their sh!t together, is charismatic, that people connect to that person, who is a great listener, organized, but also understands things, is motivated, is patient, these are often people that display and use more of their EQ skills. We've identified core and hard skills, talents, and gifts, but these work in creative ways when you exercise EQ. Including work, career, interpersonal relationships. It also applies to your awareness of these characteristics in yourself. By being aware of your profile, core values, strengths, and tendencies, you bring a greater appreciation for others as well.

A version of the emotional intelligence test (which you can access for free or opt for a paid version) asks a series of questions to find out how you react in various situations. These include:

- Stressful or frustrating situations
- Failures or discouraging situations

- Leadership positions and methods for achieving success
- Techniques for managing the emotions of others of different ages
- Methods for assessing various personality traits in others
- Dealing with diversity and cultural sensitivities

A study conducted by Forbes found that "90% of top performers also scored high in emotional intelligence, while only 20% of bottom performers scored high in emotional intelligence. This same study also found that average salary is linked to emotional intelligence. Participants with a high degree of emotional intelligence made an average of $29,000 more per year than participants with a low degree of emotional intelligence" (Bradberry, 2014).

The company Inc. also released "Ten Ways to Increase Your Emotional Intelligence" by Young Entrepreneur Council (2018), noting that these skills are aligned to support a natural progression and improvement in performance. Note: Unlike IQ, which can be highly dependent on intellectual knowledge, rationalization, and logic, EQ skills are accessible by everyone. It's a matter of practicing behavior to encourage a natural use of skills and response mechanisms. Available coaching and courses can be leveraged in this area, so that trigger points can be identified and used. Here are some key areas to work on in order to develop your EQ skills.

1. Utilize an Assertive Style of Communicating

Assertive communication goes a long way toward earning respect without coming across as too aggressive or too passive. Emotionally intelligent people know how to communicate their opinions and needs directly while still respecting others.

2. Respond Instead of Reacting to Conflict

During instances of conflict, emotional outbursts and feelings of anger are common. The emotionally intelligent person knows how to stay calm during stressful situations. They don't make impulsive decisions that can lead to even more significant problems. They understand that in times of conflict, the goal is a resolution, and they make a conscious choice to focus on ensuring that their actions and words are in alignment with that.

3. Utilize Active Listening Skills

In conversations, emotionally intelligent people listen for clarity instead of just waiting for their turn to speak. They make sure they understand what is being said before responding. They also pay attention to the nonverbal details of a conversation. Preventing misunderstandings, allows the listener to respond appropriately, and shows respect for the person they are speaking to.

4. Be Motivated

Emotionally intelligent people are self-motivated, and their attitude motivates others. They set goals and are resilient in the face of challenges.

5. Practice Ways to Maintain a Positive Attitude

Don't underestimate the power of your attitude. A negative attitude quickly infects others if a person allows it to. Emotionally intelligent people have an awareness of the moods of those around them and guard their approach accordingly. They know what they need to do to have a good day and an optimistic outlook, such as having a great breakfast or lunch, engaging in prayer or meditation during the day, or keeping positive quotes at their desk or computer.

6. Practice Self-Awareness

Emotionally intelligent people are self-aware and intuitive. They are aware of their own emotions and how they can affect those around them. They also pick up on others' feelings and body language and use that information to enhance their communication skills.

7. Take Critique Well

An essential part of increasing your emotional intelligence is to be able to take critique. Instead of getting offended or defensive, high EQ people take a few moments to understand where the commentary is coming from, how it is affecting others or their performance, and how they can constructively resolve any issues.

8. Empathize with Others

Emotionally intelligent people know how to empathize. They understand that empathy is a trait that shows emotional strength, not weakness. Empathy helps them to relate to others on a basic human level. It opens the door for mutual respect and understanding between people with differing opinions and situations.

9. Utilize Leadership Skills

Emotionally intelligent people have excellent leadership skills. They have high standards for themselves and set an example for others to follow. They take the initiative and have unique decision making and problem-solving skills – allowing for a higher and more productive level of performance in life and at work.

10. Be Approachable and Friendly

Emotionally intelligent people come off as approachable. They smile and give off a positive presence. They utilize appropriate social skills based on their relationship with whomever they are around. They have excellent interpersonal skills and know-how to communicate clearly, whether the communication is verbal or nonverbal.

Exercise: Following these steps will give you a starting point to explore this area, which will also complement and will help you polish your talents and skills. An excellent resource to take the test, and to find a multitude of educational tools, is the website the Frameworks website (See Appendix). Start by taking their self-reflecting assessment to understand your tendencies.

Later in this book, you will find an entire section dedicated to giving and contributing, as a significant step in the SmartRise process. But volunteering is also about personal growth and self-management. The primary reason why people give their time, money, or other assets is to do good for others. But in return, wow, is it rewarding! Not only do people contagiously give, which encourages more of a good behavior, but giving to others that have less … this creates a different worldview, one that contains compassion, gratitude, love, and care. I have volunteered for a mission or organization for most of my life. Today, I work with children and cannot express the feeling you get from being able to interact with these kids. Their spirit is so light, but they come with all sorts of circumstances. To be in a position of giving to a child, when I have an inner child that needs healing, brings me joy and the intention I need to work and live with purpose.

Personal growth is an evolving, iterative process that requires a great deal of honest evaluation of who you are at any given point in your life. Transitions and life events can feel harmful, or create delays in your personal growth. Note that changes in our plans are the universe's way of giving us additional tools and experiences, so that we can manage something more significant that's ahead. Growth includes understanding your energy, deepening your dialogue and nourishment of your inner child, and wrapping it all with emotional intelligence, to ensure a smooth transition through life challenges and growing pains and giving and sharing multiples your skills, relationships, and perspective. By understanding yourself along with embracing your growth progression, you're on your way to not only attracting your ideal job, but connecting yourself to a much larger plan that extends well beyond your immediate understanding. Happy growing!

Chapter 8: Step 4 – Financial Prosperity: Growing Your Assets and Career Footprint

"Success will be within your reach only when you start reaching out for it."
– Stephen Richards

The goal of this chapter is to learn to identify your financial intent, setting SMART goals, and how to use your career to achieve financial success.

Relationship with Money

At a young age, I was taught to give and not necessarily be so attached to material goods. Money cannot buy love; we all hear often. However, we're on this earth to live a human experience, and part of that experience is to work with money. Depending on where you live and the type of money-driven market you live in, your intent or relationship with money may differ.

Growing up, I was probably on the poorer side of the financial scale. However, I didn't experience a lack of food on the table, we always had a home, and, thankfully, our parents made it a priority to display an appreciation for money, but in a way that was giving and caring.

Money was a necessity for living and survival. Your upbringing, even the block you live on, often are determinants of your wealth and health. Much of my recent work in healthcare involves predicting people's engagement and behavior related to areas such as finance and health access. Unfortunately, different social factors, including your gender and race, do play a factor in wealth.

We will not go much in-depth regarding areas of wealth and financial disparities, but rather focus on how to promote growth throughout life, regardless of what we may perceive as barriers. I believe that it's important to be aware and acknowledge disparities, not so that we see them as limitations or reasons why we're falling behind in our financial success, but instead to honor those that have worked so hard to set the path for many of us today, and to drive change for ourselves and future generations.

Money is a concept of perspective and priority. It often plays a crucial role in determining the course of your career, but also in your overall wellness. Many say, "Time is money." But it's not. Money is limited, while time is infinitely accessible. From the minute we're born to our death, time never stops. It's just a matter of how we use it.

Money Matters

Take a look at the wheel of life. Where is money and wealth compared to other life areas? Wealth and career can sometimes be used interchangeably because of the strong cause-and-effect relationship they can have. However, they have very different roles to play when it comes to our fulfillment. As a child, I learned that money came from work, effort, exertion of energy. Unquestionably, one's education plays an essential role in educating us on the value of wealth, and also how to accrue assets and options.

Unfortunately, most of the US school system does not include these life topics as subjects. Most of us learned through our parents or community the basic flow of life: after college (if you're lucky) you get a job, you buy a house, and work forever, or until you retire. Concepts such as retirement funds were introduced to me when I started working for companies that offered these types of funds. One thing I did know for sure, at an early age, is that I did not, and I still do not, intend to work when I'm gracefully in my golden years. I always positioned career closer to passion and hobbies than I did to money. Many of the family members and friends required second and third jobs to make a living. It was always tied to effort.

The way I viewed this is that if I have multiple jobs, then how will I have time to spend my earnings? How will I grow so that I'm in a position of having money and other assets working for me? I have friends that love working eighty-hour weeks because their primary driver is money, and they like a lot of it. Others work eighty hours because they love their jobs, and others don't do either. I never want to worry about it, but I do appreciate a lifestyle of comfort and travel. So I see money as a conduit of convenience. Consider the appearance of the Kardashians and YouTube influencers. Their activity led to the term "self-made" becoming very popular, refer-ring to people having become successful or wealthy by one's efforts.

A 2017 survey from Fidelity Investments found that 88% of millionaires are self-made. Only 12% inherited significant money (at least 10% of their wealth). This is telling us that there's value in having a plan to reach desired financial goals while playing the dance of what you do for a living. There's a chance to achieve whatever your financial goals for all of us, it's a matter of aligning it with the things that we most value in life at any given point in our lives. You don't have to rely too heavily on winning the lottery. There's a much lesser chance of making any significant money that way than through your own efforts. So I would rather bet on you!

Exercise: Review and think through the following questions. Each one will reveal how you have learned to relate to money.

- What beliefs did you inherit from your parents in money matters?
- What do you remember the most from your childhood regarding money?
- What is the first word that comes to your mind when you hear the word "money"?
- How important is money in your life? Why do you feel that way?
- Would you take a job (you may or may not like) just for the money?
- Do you attach a monetary worth to your being? Why do you feel that way?
- Which do you value more, money or material objects?
- How do you make decisions to spend money (spontaneous, careful, do not care)?
- How do you feel about financially privileged people?
- How do you feel about financially deprived people?

It is essential to see money for what it is in order to detach any negative or positive perceptions about it. It is a means of exchange for goods. The use of and access to money and material goods impact our wellness and ability to address fundamental survival and security aspects of our life, like food, shelter, and health. Aligning to other areas of your life is the first step in prioritizing efforts that lead to financial success. There are varying degrees of success, such as accumulation of wealth, retirement funds, access to money to invest or support areas of one's life, like fun and recreation. There are also different sources and methods of achieving financial objectives, in addition to work, such as assets, passive income, and capital.

Growing and Planning for Assets

There are plenty of resources out there about how to grow and accumulate wealth. This chapter will touch upon critical aspects and traits to successfully align wealth and finances to your career plan as you transition to the new phase of your path, while providing you with resources that will stick with you forever, regardless of financial circumstances and career.

If there's a first money-talk stop, it's probably Robert Kiyosaki's *Rich Dad Poor Dad*. It's about Robert Kiyosaki and his two dads – his real father (poor dad), and the father of his best friend (rich dad) – and how both men shaped his thoughts about money and investing. The two overarching ideas are:

1. You don't need to earn a high income to be wealthy.
2. Rich people make money work for them.

Robert also expands on this by sharing the Five Big Ideas:

1. The poor and the middle-class work for money. The rich have money work for them.
2. It's not how much money you make that matters. It's how much money you keep.
3. Rich people acquire assets. The poor and middle class acquire liabilities that they think are assets.
4. Financial aptitude is what you do with money once you make it, how you keep people from taking it from you, how to keep it longer, and how you make money work hard for you.
5. The single most powerful asset we all have is our mind.

The most important lesson for me was the concept of asset versus liabilities. As Robert explains the concept, "You must know the difference between an asset and a liability, and buy assets." An asset puts money in your pocket, and liability takes money out of your pocket. The wealthy buy assets, resulting in capital, and creating more capital. The poor only have expenses. The middle class buy liabilities they think are assets.

So you mean owning a house or car is not what you need to do? For years, I thought these were primary indicators of financial success. For most of us, genuinely owning a house is not immediately accessible. We take a thirty-year loan out, give most of our savings as a down payment. This home is a liability for most of its lifespan unless its value exponentially reaches a height much higher than the original market value. A new car loses nearly 25% of the price you pay for it the moment you drive it off the lot. Yet the American dream has been engraved in so many of our brain cells that we live by this concept.

I'm not in any way discouraging owning a house or a car, but a component of your wealth planning needs to consider the appropriateness of when to buy versus lease homes and cars. There are several related tools online, and I advise you to both assess readiness and also educate yourself on options and methods that work for your path, depending on whether you have kids and their age, your total income saved, your expenses, and other assets.

Do you recall the financial crisis that began in 2007 and 2008? Weak and fraudulent underwriting practices in borrowing operations combined with high-interest rates led to many of us investing in homes without the appropriate readiness. It left many homeless, with debt, and no financial security. That same year I decided to become a business owner and invested in a recruitment company. From an early age, I was an excited entrepreneur. I love creating ideas, designing, and selling. I figured a bunch of people had been laid-off, so they would need help to find a new job, that this was the perfect business. With very little mentorship and research, I spent $30,000 purchasing the design and concept. The first mistake I made was paying someone else to run the business from day one. I retained my full-time job to make sure I had funds to pay for the company. So essentially, I created a liability flow. I got an office and a desk and called it my place of business. I had two clients.

Most importantly, because all businesses were in the process of downsizing, although I could help hundreds of people to relocate, there were no placements for them.

Supply and demand! I bring this up because it shows my inability to connect the dots with what were real assets and liabilities, but also assess how the market is behaving and reacting to news and events.

Kiyosaki's book encourages that we keep expenses low, reduce liabilities, and diligently build a base of substantial assets. According to that author, real assets fall into the following categories:

1. Stocks
2. Bonds
3. Income-generating real estate
4. Notes (IOUs)
5. Royalties from intellectual property such as music, scripts, and patents
6. Anything else that has value, produces income, or appreciates, and has a ready market

Much easier said than done. First, you need to be in a position to understand the risks associated with each category. Additionally, you need to review how to fit each segment into your plan and implement it in a way that's easiest for you to process and stick to it.

Financial Planning and Asset Development Tips

- Understand that you can have multiple sources of income, and that not all have to be from a full-time job.
- Set a financial goal. Use a financial tool to help determine, for example, how much do you want to save and how often, a vacation fund, etc. Use

SMART goals, as you have learned in earlier chapters.

- Look at your monthly expenses. Credit card tools and online tools like Mint are very good at helping you see where expenses are going.
- Assess what are musts versus nice-to-have expenses.
- According to the popular fifty-thirty-twenty rule, you should reserve 50% of your budget for essentials like rent and food, 30% for discretionary spending, and at least 20% for savings. (Credit for the fifty-thirty-twenty rule goes to Senator Elizabeth Warren, who reportedly used to teach it when she was a bankruptcy professor.)
- Consider increasing or investing in a 401K or IRA account. Having cash sitting in savings, with low rates may not bring as much capital growth over time
- Income from your job versus assets. Over time, ideally, the majority of your income should come from assets, not from labor. I'm still working on that, but I'm happy I know this now. Personally, when I recently made an incremental shift in this area, it helped me see the opportunity of not associating my career with money. We don't want to be in a position of not wanting to change toward a career or job that we may love, because of fear of financial or job insecurity. I've learned through my encounters that over time, the less stresses are associated with the other, the more fulfillment independently they bring to one's life.

"So", you may ask, "what are people doing to expand their assets? Building passive income, which:

- Increases your wealth-building plan.
- Creates an opportunity to retire early.
- Protects you from a complete loss of revenue if you lose your job.
- Provides an additional source of income when you're no longer able to work or if you outlive your retirement fund.

Note: The higher your assets, the greater the passive return. They are investments in long-term, high-interest accounts. I have mainly found the Wealth Front app to be a very convenient way to grow your cash, with very little time investment on my part. Don't fall for any passive income ideas that promise a quick return or require vast amounts of money upfront. They will sabotage your other financial goals, and are probably not trustworthy. Look for methods that are steady, profitable, and trustworthy. Do your research. And never go into debt!

Building Passive Income

What can we consider as passive income? There are plenty of options. It can start with more traditional accounts, but usually, leveraging what others prefer not to do on their own is a great starting point. Here are some ideas:

Investment and Retirements Funds: 401K and high-interest long-term accounts. As I mentioned, I have mainly found Wealth Front tool to be a very convenient way to both grow your cash, with an option to contribute from my assets automatically.

Start a blog or a YouTube channel: If you have a brilliant idea that appeals to a specific audience, you could create something like an educational blog or a YouTube tutorial series to generate online traffic. If your content is engaging and it sees enough daily traffic, you could sell ad space on your blog or ad spots on your channel. After you put in the heavy lifting, you can sit back, relax, and enjoy streams of passive income.

Sell digital products: If you've discovered how to create content that produces enough traffic to host ads, you could make a product your audience would love to buy. That could be anything from a simple e-book to a sophisticated app that generates income for years after it's released.

Store people's stuff: People have a lot of stuff – and they're always looking for inexpensive ways to store it. What could be easier than having people pay you to store their stuff? Building passive income by offering storage could involve a large-scale investment of buying a storage facility (with cash!) or something simpler, like providing your basement or shed. You'll need to ensure their items are safe and secure.

Rent out useful items: Do you have any items that you don't use all the time, that others would like to borrow? Useful things like a truck, trailer, trampoline, kayak, or even your yard could earn you passive income as rental items, including renting out spare rooms in your house with the help of websites like Airbnb. Hop on your favorite social media site, upload pictures of your items, set a price, and tell the world they're ready for rent.

Financial Freedom

A must-read in the area of sustainable and consistent wealth growth is John Soforic's *The Wealthy Gardener* (2018). The book is a hybrid (half-fiction, half non-fiction), and it beautifully provides practical ways to accumulate growth and obtain financial freedom. Each lesson can be applied to any area of your life and speaks clearly to the areas where most people fall short. Throughout the series of lessons, Soforic nicely reveals the core of what for me has been an internal tug of war as it relates to my understanding of money: "Prosperity is the power to take a walk in the woods on a weekday, pay for college tuitions, and live with choices, options, and power. It is awakening without money worries. It is living without the pressure of time. It is the ability to experience one's daily hours in meaningful pursuits. And it required me to grow spiritually in the struggle. Be wary of those who tell you to be content with your conditions in life. Only you can know the conditions that will satisfy your soul. And only you can feel the pull of your ambition." (Soforic, 2018, pg. 5).

In particular, note that he says, "be wary of those who tell you to be content with your conditions in life." I've always found it exciting to balance between keeping life priorities in order and maintaining gratitude and achieving financial wealth. Up to this date, I still hear people telling me, "Don't kill yourself at work," or, "Why do you work so hard?" During my twenties, I must admit that I learned to use work as an escape, while understanding that I needed to put in the time in my career, while I was young and had less expenses. I completely understand everyone's concern; however, I'm enjoying how I'm investing my time.

In his book, Soforic describes the importance of how you use free time. I think of it as time in general. Essentially, he outlines that you shouldn't expect riches and growth without any investment in time. That applies to anything that you considered necessary. Remember: You don't have to keep the same priorities throughout your life. During my twenties, it was about career and financial growth; that shifted during my late twenties to personal growth, fun and recreation; my early thirties were about spirituality and family. As I move into my mid-thirties, it's about my relationship with my husband and financial freedom, because soon enough, the priority will turn back to family, as we grow our family together. This priority shifting does not result in other areas neglected, but shifts the attention they get; if something has to give, it will likely not be my top three. Also, I find value in rotating my wheels of life. Each area builds healthy, active habits that set me up for the next stage in my life.

The second lesson that resonates with me is the power of keeping your deepest desires as close as possible to you. Soforic describes how he kept his book writing a secret because he didn't want to hear an opinion that might remotely steer him in a different direction. As I write, very few people know about this book. I have followed my gut on this one. For similar reasons, I, too, believe that even those who have the highest intentions for you sometimes, may say things like, "Why are you spending time writing this book?", or, "You have so many things already on your plate." Because I choose not to hear that, and it doesn't lift me in any way, and, more importantly, because I see the value in investing this time for a much greater good that extends beyond me, this book has been somewhat incubated.

Why Giving Leads to Wealth

The last lesson to share in this chapter is about the impact of giving. It's often a misconception that if you feel you don't have enough, you're unable to give. If you give, you will receive. Gifting and giving come in the form of time, emotion, action, and money. Feeling rich is not just an accumulation of wealth, and giving can occur in any format. When it comes to wealth, there's power in spreading your wealth to others. Describing someone as rich, is less of a monetary attribute. In reality, I see it as someone who is confident in his or her values and shares them. One that smiles at someone and means it. A person that expresses gratitude and kindness and has dreams, experiencing freedom as they work towards those dreams. One who's disciplined because they trust. A person who loves and surrenders to that, that's greater than themselves. This notion doesn't take away the roadblocks and human emotions we might feel along the way to wealth.

I sense that giving connects us to a broader mission, and allows us to practice things like gratitude, which brings back a sense of personal fulfillment. Indeed, research has shown that giving leads to wealth.:

Giving increases your sense of wealth: In the study, "I Give, Therefore I Have: Giving and Subjective Wealth" by Zoe Chance of Yale University and Michael Norton of Harvard Business School (2011), it was observed that giving away money increases the giver's "sense of wealth," psychologically. It makes sense that you feel wealthier when you give. Granted, the majority of us aren't satisfied with our financial situation but contributing to save lives and help the less privilege creates a sense of wealth.

Giving also increases your happiness: Nothing supersedes the feeling of happiness and fulfillment that comes from giving to the less privileged. For most of us, much of daily life is vain, and we know it; the little happiness and fulfillment derived from giving to others, no matter the amount or frequency, can make a whole lot of difference in our lives.

Giving Increases Your Productivity: A happy man is a more productive man; there's no doubt about it. Giving increases your happiness, which leads to fulfillment and a sense of purpose, which in turn increases your productivity in day-to-day activities.

Increased happiness and productivity lead to increased income or wealth: The increased happiness and productivity you experience then leads to increased income and wealth for you.

Exercise: Write yourself a check for your future self. In a few sentences, answer the following: How did you earn it? How will you use it? How will you celebrate or reward yourself for receiving it? With it, write a gratitude letter.

Throughout this chapter, you have learned valuable tips on how to increase your wealth. Like with any goal and anything that's prioritized, having a plan is critical. Be sure that you are competent in skills of accumulating wealth as you transition and build up your career. You will see the value of applying these principles to ensure your assets continue growing with time. You want to be able to withstand any unexpected or unplanned volatility that's outside of your control and influence, the areas you do have control over, as Covey taught us. Be sure to:

Be disciplined. People that consistently follow their plan and adjust their goals as demanded by their natural progression in life, whether that means sticking to their budget or savings goals.

Be confident: Know and trust that your plan will work. People who keep their eyes on the prize respond the best to stressful times they may impact them financially, like layoffs and other life events, like marriage and children. Sure there will be times of loss, and also windfalls, but believe that you will achieve your dreams.

Manage your time wisely: As we learned from Soforic, how you use your free time determines growth. This of this time as planting seeds and cultivating a garden. We all have the same twenty-four hours, and yet we experience such a significant difference in output. Growth requires steady steps toward achieving higher levels of roles, positions within their industry, or organization such as personal development, educational enhancement, and anything that will lead to more significant impact to your productivity and self-management.

Be humble. Keep your relationship with the material world in check as it is there for convenience, not fulfillment. Give and know that you will receive, multiplied.

Chapter 9:
Step 5 – Connecting with Yourself: The Best Approach to Your Career Plan

"We are not human beings having a spiritual experience. We are spiritual beings having a human experience."
– Pierre Teilhard de Chardin

You have now reached a core component of your book career journey. Here you will learn how to design your career plan with purpose, action, and balance by tapping into their inner resources as a source of guidance and wisdom.

Your Higher Power

To understand spirituality and its connection with our inner being, we must understand the meaning of love. Second, we must acknowledge a Higher Power not as sitting and looking down from heaven, but instead the source of love and wisdom that we breathe and carry within us.

Osho wrote, "Only at the highest peak, when love is not a relationship anymore, when love becomes a state of your being, the lotus opens totally, and great perfume is released – but only at the highest peak. At the lowest, love is just a political relationship. At the highest, love is a religious state of consciousness. I love you, too. Buddha loves, Jesus loves, but their love demands nothing in return. Their love is given for the sheer joy of giving it; it is not a bargain. Hence, the radiant beauty of it, hence the transcendental beauty of it. It surpasses all the joys that you have known". Visit <u>Osho's website</u> (See Appendix) for more information.

Love is freedom, and it's whole. It needs nothing in return and has no expectations. It's not disappointed. We often tie it to relationships and even our careers and jobs. But love for our jobs is not in the job. It's the thought, the feeling of joy, and actions that come from putting our authentic self into gear. It's an energy that touches every form and aspect of our lives, manifesting through the fulfillment of our path.

My husband is a vivid reflection of the power of inner connection. He's a unique spirit filled with adventures and vibrancy. I visualize him and don't see his face and body, but a bunch of colors bursting with excitement – the energy and enthusiasm of a child. I love his pure heart and sincerity. For the first time, someone other than myself has connected the way my husband has to my inner self, because he loves all aspects of me, and he is able to communicate with them. Similarly, with our jobs, it may not be about the function, role or title; rather, it's the interactions, the non-tangible return, such as engagement, knowledge, creativity. The overall return and connection to your core values.

The only requirement for love is tapping into yourself, the most significant source of love. Connecting with your High Power is getting to know love.

"Courage is the hallmark of spirituality. Courage comes when you love yourself for who you are."
– Amit Ray.

Tapping into our inner guides and Higher Powers promotes the strength and courage we will need to gain perspective and attitude only carried when we truly know love. Regardless of our spiritual journey – religious or non-religious – this applies to all. Through our thoughts, we create our heaven and hell. We're the creators of our journey and tuning into our natural state allows us to follow our natural path. It may be days, months, and even years before we realize the power of our thoughts, and actions, but we will eventually realize that we have been the creator of our own reality.

Take nature, for instance. When I look around and think of nature, walking in the park, beautiful oak trees, the seasons that exist throughout the world at any given time, the air we breathe each morning, and how specific body functions work without us consciously thinking about it, like your heart and circulation, breathing, and how particular areas of your brain light up when you're excited or sad, or painting and doing your budget, I sense that we're so perfectly designed to function. When we travel, I admire the mechanics of an airplane, the beauty, and the tallness of the cities and the fantastic advances in technology.

Then wonder that there are so many, many more things we don't see. Therefore, we probably don't understand them fully. As I look forward to the lives touched by this book, for example, and how my life has played out over time, and how each event (happy or unhappy) is so beautifully connected, I've concluded that there's something way beyond anything we understand. Going through life on your own, not necessarily understanding yourself all the time, and yet finding a purpose, can be very complicated, and acknowledging that there's something more significant, a bigger plan, explains the intricacies of those invisible somethings.

The way I imagine this scenario is like a video game. The video game has a designer. The game has different characters that have different strengths and profiles. They each play a role, there are several paths based on the decisions and sources each character decides to play, but there's also a story line, and you as the main character have a purpose. In a video game, usually, the objective is given upfront, and throughout the game, you gain points or powers that allow you to advance to other unexplored areas. But ultimately, there's an end game. The more you play the character, the more you become familiar with the maneuvers you can make to be successful at going to the next phase.

There's an equivalent scenario in life. I refer to a Higher Power as the internal asset we have from the power that brought us to this world. People use different ways of tapping into their Higher Power through prayer, meditation, and other relaxation techniques. If you think of human birth, the entire process is quite a miracle, and we're each so blessed to be here. I have made it my mission to play my character to my purpose; anything else becomes less satisfying.

What's your Higher Power? If you don't know, I invite you to close your eyes after you read and follow these instructions. Imagine yourself in your most relaxed position. We're going to your happy place. Where are you? Who are you with, or are you by yourself? Are you standing or sitting? Now imagine something or someone that feels loving, caring, empathetic, accessible at all times, safe, loyal, patient, responsible, filled with knowledge, compassionate, and trustworthy is there. What is it? Is it a person? A feeling? An object? Or space? A group? If it speaks to you? What is it saying? Touch your Higher Power and look at it. "Until next time", you say. Use this visualization each time you connect to foster a relationship with your Higher Power. Just like your inner child, it will answer questions. Unlike your inner child, the Higher Power lives outside of your wounds, and your behavior toward it does not torment it. Instead, it will always have compassion and love for you. You are its precious creation.

Exercise: Each day, as you write your ten things you are grateful for, think and feel your Higher Power. It will help you not only deepen your relationship, but also to acknowledge the fact that the things you are grateful for result from a place that's greater than yourself.

Spirituality in Motion

If you recall from my personal story, the moments I felt the most connected with myself, most fulfilled, were as a child when I prayed, and then as an adult, when I did it more consistently. I pray for clarity and wisdom these days. I'm never that specific because, in reality,

I don't necessarily know what outcomes are indeed the best for me. I've learned that sometimes, the things I desired maybe seemed reasonable, but then something even more significant happened, or the result I wanted led to misery.

Instead, I pray to pose the issue or concern and guidance on how to address it. I pray for others' wellbeing, and throughout the day, I connect to be more grateful than ever. I noticed the areas of my life that I'm most thankful for are also the ones with the highest strength. One growing area for me is my ability to remember more often to connect with my Higher Power throughout the day. As mundane as it might sound, go for it. Don't wait until you have a health issue, or you experience a period of grief. Your Higher Power will guide your decisions, thoughts, and actions. Just like the main character in the video game, it gains more strength, the more you know how to access it, even if that means going through "game over" multiple times.

Your current and future career or job is grounds for a spiritual journey. It is the place where you must take each opportunity to be the person you are, your authentic self. The ones who bring its unique magic and gifts to the workplace are those who truly work to their highest potential. Use your Higher Power to navigate your strengths, talents, and core values. You will start recognizing this feeling, "I did my job today!", when you have tapped into a hard or soft skill that leads you to achieve a higher purpose beyond your own.

For example, I came to my office at 7:30 a.m. I was able to shift someone's perspective on an issue, and the same person tells me by 8:03 a.m., "I always feel better when I talk to you. Your confidence is contagious." At that point, I hear something inside me tell me, "You're done for the day!" It certainly wasn't the end of the day. But in reality, I met the higher purpose, and that's what will lead you, too, to the ultimate real end game. Those of us who can have more of those moments throughout our day as part of a career are truly blessed.

As you seek to transition and as you formulate your career plan, connect with a Higher Power. Don't be discouraged if you're currently in a job that may be draining or discouraging today. If it's your "real" job, that's the one you must accomplish each day. It will provide you with confirmation and also guidance in a way that speaks to you. Recall that, for me, that means I often see the number three in sequence. When I think of what I was thinking about those specific moments, I know I have received a confirmation or blessing to keep moving along. One of the things that becomes very apparent when we are connected with Higher Power is that we are inherently pleased and satisfied.

What's a Chakra?

The more your desire to be connected grows, the more you want to seek information that gives you more connection. Soon after my divorce, I was a total, unbalanced mess. The world seemed right and wrong at the same time, and I remember encountering an article that led me to exploring chakras and how they influence the energy that navigates the body. My life hasn't been the same since. _Chakras_ are described as "the circular vortexes of energy that are placed in seven different points on the spinal column, and all the *seven chakras* are connected to the various organs and glands within the body."

Chakras drive energy through several areas and functions of your being, including your physical properties, anatomy, and emotional connections. Fulfillment is high-level term, but when we're able to deep dive into its meaning and evolution especially in our careers and jobs, we're talking about each of the areas below that our chakras' energy manifests, when fully balanced and functional.

The body is correctly connected to its surroundings, air, and earth, because it, too, is formed of energy. I used to hear the term "imbalanced" and genuinely didn't have an understanding of what it meant. Now I see that, as with any vortex or circulating motion, energy can turn at a different frequency, often referred to as blocked chakras. When chakras are blocked, other areas or chakras compensate for the other's lack of energy flow.

Exercise: Below are the descriptions of balanced, blocked, and overactive chakras. Check to see in what state your chakras are flowing.

- Know that you are secure and stable, that you have a connection with you are inner-self and are aware of your authentic self (root chakra).
- Feel and express pleasure and creativity (sacral chakra).
- Confidently take action, feel empowered, and drive change (solar plexus chakra).
- Love what you do and apply love and compassion throughout your day in decisions and daily functions (heart chakra).

- Express and communicate your thoughts, creativity, and others' ability to perceive your authentic self (throat chakra).
- Use your emotional intelligence to engage, execute, and deliver (third-eye chakra).
- Understand your real function and role by using your inner guides and Higher Power (crown chakra).

Tapping into Your Inner Connection

Our body, mind, and spirit compensate for remaining in balance all the time, and this manifests in our relationships, workload, even our physical bodies – if one leg hurts, a lot of pressure is placed on the other. At the end of it all, the world is complete, our life is whole, and each movement's actions contribute to the whole. When I learned about Chakras, I quickly learned about Reiki. I was in such great transition of all types, work, relationships … I also moved, all in a matter of months, and it became apparent to me that I needed time to reconnect with myself. Connecting with my Higher Power or myself were only concepts to me. That's usually the case for most of us. In my research about chakras on how to unblock or enhance their movement, I found Reiki.

Reiki is a relaxation technique that promotes healing through light touch. Reiki is made of two Japanese words – Rei, which means "God's Wisdom or the Higher Power" and Ki, which is "life force energy." The first time I was exposed to it, I was having a relentless, tough time letting go of old feelings and of a relationship that was not available to me. I had an enormous backache, to the point I could barely walk. I remember walking into the practitioner's beautiful apartment, knowing that I was in for a treat. She warned me that my life would never be the same again, and boy, was she right, in all the right ways. Reiki not only brought me to a state of stillness and silence but to a place that felt safe, compassionate, one that focused on self-care and kindness. It was when I connected to my Higher Power, so that I knew what that meant.

The beauty of Reiki is that it doesn't stop with the technique or session. You see the effects of it before and after. Whenever I go to a Reiki session, I can feel each of my chakras spinning with heat. Everyone has a different experience, and for me, it brings me back to my authentic self., the place that allows me to be free and allows me to manifest the best version of myself out there in the world. I started practicing self-Reiki healing at home as my way of continuing to practice self-care at my own time.

Throughout your career transition, you are essentially removing yourself from the past, grounding and centering yourself in what it is you need today so that you can plan for the future, without necessarily obsessing over the outcomes. It requires a leap of faith that things will feel better for an extended period, and that the transition aligns with all areas of your life. Having faith can be a big ask, but one that, once connected to your Higher Power, will come naturally.

And with Reiki, I started seeing a difference at work, especially. There was a sense of ease with what needed to happen. There's nothing more powerful than knowing you're exactly where you need to be, and that wisdom is available to you at all times whenever you need a guiding voice, or in my case, numbers, to make sure your track is clear.

You will encounter the roadblocks and challenges that will prepare you for the next phase. It's the universe's way of preparing you for future ease, that's all. When you realize this, then your response to life becomes more of accepting energy. When we resist, we struggle. In this struggle, we're rejecting the universe's gift that exists to facilitate wisdom and personal growth, to help us learn. Without these challenges, we don't build strength, and life will accumulate difficulties ahead that your character will not tolerate. Like a character from my video game, you must beat the boss to gain access to the sword, which you'll need in the next course to open the door to the magic kingdom.

"Who Do You Want to Be?" Is the Real Question

Instead of walking through life wondering what you want to do, let's ask, "Who do you want to *be*?" This is truly the question that must be asked as you become in tune with your purpose and mission. So many times, I see people specifying what they want to *do*, like becoming a finance department director or the chief of staff at a well-established franchise. Although, that's a significant step toward developing a pathway, it's not the only component of your career mapping that plays a role in your overall fulfillment. Understand instead who you want to be as a person, such as compassionate, energetic, a leader, or creative driver of excellence and change. Those may be the qualities of the person you may want to be. Your job, then, becomes the opportunity for you to orchestrate yourself beyond just a title or role, but the highest part of yourself, and the plan that extends well beyond the organization or career. It's the role of your spirit and energy.

Going beyond the title and the role requires ego release. The ego is the conscious mind. Its purpose is to rationalize and be logical and comes in different shapes and forms. It protects and defends us from harm or feeling unpleasant feelings, and it wants us to feel good about ourselves. The ego is not specific in terms of how it gets us there, so if you don't lead with your authentic self, it seeks tools from the material world. When we notice that we are about to feel hurt, we may get tense, which distracts us from feeling the pain. When we are not feeling relaxed, we are usually avoiding some unpleasant feeling or several feelings. We can also deny feeling something. This defensiveness makes us very concerned with the outside of us, with how we appear to other people. It makes it harder to notice what goes on inside of us, with our inner feelings. The result of all these defensive tactics is that we're not really in touch with ourselves. We don't *know* ourselves when we don't *feel* ourselves. Consequently, we are unaware of why we are doing things; thus, the ego becomes the mastermind behind our self-identity.

For me, releasing the ego has been and continues to be an ongoing effort. I'm your typical over-achiever; that's okay if the desire to achieve is for your self-accomplishment; however, there's a fine line between self-accomplishment and the expectation of reward. These days more consistently, I aim for personal fulfillment, not with the expectation of a work recognition or even gratitude. My goal is to meet a higher purpose and experience gratitude in the process.

Understanding the dynamics, balance and interactions that chakras have on your body, mind and spirit will help you better feel your natural state, a state that's complex, yet practical, and one of optimal performance, growth and centeredness. Going for Reiki sessions is one of my mechanisms of experiencing the symptoms of connectedness, one that serves as a reminder of how great it feels to be me, with no obligations, prioritizing your mind and spirit, where nothing other than spirit exists in the world, and the body is filled only with its own energy, not requiring external approvals, gratifications or influence.

Finding Your Path

"Make your own Bible. Select and collect all the words and sentences that in all your readings have been to you like the blast of a trumpet."
– Ralph Waldo Emerson

Regardless of your religion or spiritual path, being in touch with one's inner strength is a type of Higher Power. It releases the necessary wisdom and strength to plow through the many challenges our days bring us. I have learned that living through a path of connection with my own village, with resources, and with beauty the universe has shared with all of us, I have created my standards of living. There are so many religions out there, and I genuinely believe they seek the same endpoint, that of living in greatness and highest power. The path, however, may differ for each seeker. There lies the opportunity to create a spiritual path that works for you. Doing so releases any opinions, good versus bad thoughts, and perceptions that you may have developed over time. Those who think that we're flying solo in this world will struggle. Realizing that you're living a human experience, with a purpose that continually polishes through your authentic person is probably the most meaningful lesson to share with you. From there on, it's up to you to use the unlimited resources and tools available to you.

Exercise: While at work or outside, make time to think about your core values, talents, and strengths. Perform three actions that you envision the person you are or are becoming will also perform.

Meditation

The world is blessed to have gurus continuously educating, inspiring, and transforming us to become a better version of ourselves. Their gifts and talents lie in the ability to understand and connect us with these resources in a unique way. They become pillars and change agents of our journey. I have a few that I would like to share with you. One is Deepak Chopra. Deepak is a well-known advocate of alternative medicine, wellness, and personal transformation. I first encountered Deepak through the Oprah Winfrey twenty-one-day meditation series. Meditation opens the capacity for you to create your reality with purpose and life intent. Meditation, to me, started as a way to quiet my mind, but I was never able to stop my thoughts. I also had a tough time staying still and didn't enjoy it, because it was a constant resistance between what I understood meditation to be and what, in reality, was happening to my body.

When I first completed twenty-one consecutive days of meditation, my world had changed. Chopra's meditations combine education, awareness, and silence as you repeat the centering thought. Through meditation, I connect with a real feeling and have the ability of being okay with my acknowledged thoughts and letting go of things, people, and values that no longer serve me. It was about recognizing my position in relation to the rest of the world, while understanding that we all have a unique role to a larger purpose. It was one of the first times I recognized and felt the word "awareness". I learned that once you become aware of the infinite possibilities and the power that exists within you, you become unstoppable.

As we go on through our career, we're conditioned to think about promotions and growth, titles and money, and it's easy to think linearly, assuming that it's a straight shot with many external contingencies. That means relying on all the stars to align, including assuming it is others' responsibility to open up different opportunities for you, for others to recognize how creative or dependable you are. You become accustomed to serving others, hoping as a result that your needs are also met. When in reality, *you are the source of power*.

We are blessed to have each other. But it starts with understanding yourself, so that you give the best of yourself. You are the person who seeks and obtains growth, and that will be seen and supported by the right people. You are the person that accesses the right challenges to foster growth, and that means who you are and who you are becoming.

Recently I have become more and more disciplined with my meditation schedule. When I pray and meditate,

I feel like I'm at my center. Unnecessary baggage is left behind, and I feel more focused. This is the version of myself I want to bring each day to work. The more I help others, which is one of my core values, the more I'm able to enhance my human experience on earth while excelling at my daytime job. If you recall, the more aligned you become with your inner state, the clearer the messages from the universe and love become. Right before starting to write this book, and especially after, I remember waking up every night between 3 and 4 a.m. Like clockwork. One night, in particular, my now-husband was away on a business trip, and in the middle of the night, I was dreaming someone was calling my name. I heard, "Vanessa". It was a smooth, caring voice. I look at the time it was 3:33 a.m. As you know, these numbers are a confirmation that I'm not alone in venturing out on my journey.

For almost two months, I would wake up at similar times, and I would look forward to it. It gave me a feeling of security, as if someone, my Higher Power, was watching over me and supporting and guiding me every step of the way. When you know it's beyond you, you remove unnecessary weight, and your mission becomes more transparent. Each time I wake up, I embrace it and don't try to fall asleep like I used to. Instead, I started meditating, asking my inner guides to share the message that's ready for download for me. Random things come up that many times don't apply right at the moment, but reveal themselves soon after, as a confirmation. Confirmations occur when you're connected, trusting, you start seeing, hearing, feeling, all your senses are enhanced. It's not a sixth sense. It's way better. All of you is enhanced because you're working from a place within. The outside world is minimized by comparison, and using it as a source of guidance leads to misconceptions, and steers in the direction of meaningless or material desires that may only bring very short-term fulfillment.

During my 3 a.m. wakeup calls, as I now call them, I would often ask if writing a book was the right idea. I received a "duh" as a response. My inner guide has an amusing sense of humor, which makes sense, because I have a more serious side that needs to learn to chill. See if your inner guide also meets you right where you are, in a way that speaks to you.

Good Things Lead to Better Things

Goodness is like a magnet. As I learned about meditation and over time made it my routine that fits my goals, I also was inspired to write. Not necessarily writing literature, but "brain dumping", or mindless writing. Imagine when an infant speaks to you, and you understand nothing. To him or her, I'm sure it's a combination of random thoughts and expressed feelings in the purest of ways, which an adult wouldn't understand. So my inner guides speak to me similarly, but the beauty of it is that I *do* know! When I put pen to paper and write whatever combination of words, nothing has to make sense. It's a matter of accepting a great deal of information revealed.

The last time I did mindless writing was right after my most recent Akashic Records reading. I asked my Higher Power, "How can I get closer to generosity, giving, compassion, and charity that came up as part of my spiritual and career path? " When I started writing, it was like diarrhea of information. Even drawings came into play. One phrase had circles and arrows pointing at it. *Write a book.* The other one was *resting*, to allow space for creativity. Since then, I've taken over four weeks off, and I'm grateful. Otherwise, I would be neglecting my inner child, who's been begging for some quiet time. I've never felt more connected. The more you practice this connection, your path to a job, or career choices you make over the time, we'll reflect a combination of where you need to be and a strong alignment with your purpose. Your chakras will be spinning with excitement.

Yoga

"The resting place of the mind is the heart. The only thing the mind hears all day is clanging bells and noise and argument, and all it wants is quietude. The only place the mind will ever find peace is inside the silence of the heart. That's where you need to go."
— Elizabeth Gilbert

A natural progression to meditation and grounding exercise is yoga. I moved to Brooklyn just over two years ago, and we found a center of wellness, The Awakening NY, that provides yoga, Pilates, and healing exercises. Their stated mission is,"to bring health and well-being to you as a radiant manifestation of a balanced body, mind, and spirit…treatments provide nourishment for you as a whole being, the perfect being that you are." Isn't this beautiful?

I would've never understood this without experiencing the bruises, scars, and love and compassion that the universe has shared with me. As I mentioned, I often receive Reiki treatments. I often refer to it as a message for the soul, with its impact before and after. That, in combination with my yoga practice, has helped me stay centered. It's the one hour of the day where the only priority is me. For that one hour, when you're in a room with others seeking to benefit from the wonders of yoga, you find that you're connected. You're connected through gratitude, love, and care for yourself and others. There are undoubtedly physical benefits too, which I'll share later in the book, and it certainly helps you separate the mundane from what's meaningful. It reminds you that you carry yourself to everyone, and it's essential to appreciate that most significant asset, as learned early on.

Yoga has become a staple of my spiritual journey, and I will be forever grateful for the fantastic instructions my body can absorb, as each is specially designed for me. The instructors may have other jobs and obligations; however for me, they perform one of their spiritual jobs when we're in that room together. This is how the magic of authenticity multiples. We each perform our spiritual duty; we share and inspire growth and compassion and others, and then we repeat with ourselves and others. It's so important to live in the moment and keep the space open for it.

Connecting with Who You Are

The most important lesson is to be courageous enough to connect with love. Joel Osteen, an inspiring pastor and author, has been a tremendous influence on my ability to communicate with my Higher Power. The beauty of a Higher Power is that it's not specific to religions or beliefs; instead, it is a connection to your inner wisdom, source and energy that manifests into a language that speaks to you. I subscribed to his daily messages over seven years ago, and regularly, his message speaks to me like clockwork. In particular, this next message is one that I want to share with you:

"Today, many people are walking around not knowing who they really are – not naturally speaking, of course, but spiritually speaking. Once you receive Jesus Christ as your personal Lord and Savior, you take on a new identity – His identity. Everything He is, you become. Because Jesus is an overcomer, you are an overcomer (1 John 4:4). Because Jesus is more than a conqueror, you are more than a conqueror (Romans 8:37). You become empowered to do all things through Christ who gives you strength (Philippians 4:13)! Let these words sink down deep in your heart today. Realize that because of Jesus, there is greatness inside you. As you study and meditate on the Word of God, you will realize your true potential. You'll discover who you really are so you can live the good life to which He has called you!" (*Today's Word with Joel & Victoria, 2019*)

It's incredible that, once you're open to receiving abundance and understand love, it flows. As I was writing this book, most of his messages were messages I need to hear to encourage my focus and to have a clear mind to express the real message I needed to share with you. Your Higher Power is the source of love, wisdom, and compassion, to not only direct your steps, but to help you understand yourself better each step along the way.

Exercise: Ask your inner self what you can do differently today to better connect with your Higher Power. Reflect on the results of your chakras assessment, and use a SMART goal statement to describe the best way to tap into your inner resources and guidance, moving toward your understanding of your purpose and approach to your career path. Review each step in your plan, and check if that link *feels* right to you. Then modify, as necessary.

For example, your response from Higher Power is to treat others with kindness and compassion, and when performing your chakra assessment, you notice that both your solar plexus and throat chakras feel imbalanced, leading to feeling anxious and arrogant. Your goal may be to, prioritize relationships at work, because these play an important role in how effective you are in achieving your work objectives. You will establish stronger relationships at work, beginning next week, by practicing compassion and kindness towards co-workers. You will listen more attentively. You will ask for their feedback in 3 months, to see if these steps made a meaningful impact to your colleagues.

Our ability to connect to our Highest Power provides the greatest source, which allows us to innately follow the steps and approach most appropriate to us. External guidance and feedback helps us become aware of techniques and knowledge, but ultimately, how we use our resources is best guided through our individual source. When navigating the raging waters of career planning, whether it's understanding our purposes, what occupation we should focus on, or how many hours to work, tapping into source helps us design the career that not only suits us best today, but one that is all encompassing of who we are today and are ultimately becoming tomorrow, following a larger purpose that will benefit humanity as a whole.

Chapter 10:
Step 6 – Relationships:
Influence a Larger Career Purpose

"We are all connected. To each other, biologically.
To the earth, chemically. To the rest of the universe
atomically."
– Neil DeGrasse Tyson

We learned from previous chapters the power of understanding and connecting to our inner self to live our real purpose. This chapter will explore the potential of connecting to others' inner journey so that together there's power and compassion in the role that we each play toward achieving a higher plan together. You will learn the power of relationships and how they influence your career path, as well as how together we achieve a higher purpose.

"The one you are looking for is the one who is
looking."
– Francis of Assisi

In this chapter, we will learn about the one thing that's a requirement for a relationship to flourish: knowing who we really are. While there is a natural tendency to find an identity in our roles in life – our personality, work, body, culture, stories of the past, and dreams for the future – in reality, these are all temporary, external aspects of ourselves. Who we really are is eternal and unbounded. Our true self is pure love and pure spirit.

The Mirror

*"We do not see things as they are.
We see them as we are."*
– The Talmud

I recently learned about Deepak Chopra's mirror of relationships. This is the idea that all of our relationships are a reflection of ourselves. The qualities and traits we react to strongly in others reveal the attributes and qualities in us that need further understanding and balancing. The people we are attracted to are those who have the traits that we have, only more so.

Exercise: The Mirror

Step 1: Think about someone you find attractive. On the left side of a piece of paper, list ten or more qualities that you love in that person. Write quickly. The secret is not to give your conscious mind time to edit your thoughts. You can put down as many qualities as you wish, but don't stop until you have at least ten.

Step 2: Now focus on somebody who irritates you, annoys you or makes you uncomfortable in some way. Why does this person infuriate you so much? On the right side of the paper, list ten or more of their undesirable qualities.

Step 3: Look at your list for the person you find attractive and circle the three qualities that you find most appealing about him or her. Then look at the list on the right side of the paper and circle the three qualities you find most repulsive. Now read the six words you circled out loud. You, too, possess these qualities.

Notice if your perspective has recently changed about the person, that is, you found them appealing, and all of a sudden, they annoy you. In previous chapters, I had advised to leave it alone, because you may be going through a transition and do not want to disrupt the process. So this exercise is best performed when you have clarity and can objectively perform the mirror test. You will know when the time is right. Then keep in mind the result for future triggers.

Once you see yourself in others, you will find it much easier to connect with them, which ultimately helps to maintain your emotional well-being.

"You must be the change that you wish to see
in the world."
– Mahatma Gandhi

The secret of attraction is remarkably simple. We bring to us that which is similar to the quality of our thoughts and feelings. However, the most crucial factor of success in attracting what you want is to desire it from the silence of pure awareness. Only from this state of consciousness will the desire be in accord with all of nature and have the power and intelligence of the cosmos behind it. Your true nature is love, joy, and wisdom. When you experience and know that, you will attract love, joy, and knowledge into your life.

Trying to attract a relationship or a situation based only on the ego may bring some limited results, but it will not be fulfilling, long-lasting, or in your best spiritual interests, because the ego-mind comes from a state of lack and limited understanding.

Relationship Roles

In the context of empowerment and influence, relationships play three significant roles:

1. Self-awareness – through your relationship with yourself.
2. Knowledge and support – how we each learn from each other's experiences, talents, and gifts; how we use our network to lift us and together work toward a single vision.
3. Connectivity to the universe – how our relationships connect to other areas of our lives, and how together relationships multiply the abundance of growth and resources toward achieving a greater mission.

Building strong interpersonal relationships is key to our personal and career growth; this may include your life partner, family, friends, co-workers, colleagues, even your pets. Everyone has their person, and then we each play a role in other's lives. Some of these will become your biggest cheerleaders, mentors, and coaches. Others will become a barrier. Some of these relationships are there to stay, and you will outgrow others. Relationship evolvement starts with each person and the way they perceive the world, and then becoming synchronized with each other, connecting to our inner selves to serve a purpose. High-performing teams and strong romantic relationships often display complementary and diverse competencies that ultimately make them very capable of achieving the organization's , or household's mission, respectively.

We were all born into families and circumstances that were determined for us, and understanding our roots, similar to connecting with our inner child, exposes traumas and behavior that led to where we are today. Throughout my upbringing, I shared how I was often misunderstood, experienced a sense of emptiness through most of my life, and was challenged for most of that time, because I was not able to see why I felt as I did.

That was until I met Marine. Marine Sélénée is a terrific family constellations therapist (she is New York-based, but with web options for her services). In case you're ever confused about how to live to your talent, Marine is the walking story. The family constellations method that Marine uses is "placement", to understand the relationship with your roots, prior generations, and how it influences your life. My first experience in working with Marine was in a group setting. I cannot describe the process in detail, because I would love for you to experience it for yourself. However, it connected the influence that my mother has in my life, which explains why I'm the "quiet" energy or "in-my-own-world" child of the family.

I was conceived soon after my maternal grandmother had passed away. The fact that I was born mostly into a climate of death, basically created a cord between myself and feeling a loss. No wonder emptiness was a constant. The feeling of emptiness convinced me that I was always missing something. That's huge. From my story, you learned, although I love my mom, she has imposed many of her wounds on me. Especially the way I perceived my physical beauty, my hair, my weight. Words carry weight, and for better or worse, you start believing things when you hear them so often. I've learned to keep a healthy distance between my mom and myself for me to respect and love her.

We all deserve that opportunity. You may have come from a family or generations of emotional abuse or domestic violence. You, too, can heal from those wounds. Being aware of those generational patterns allows us to reset and create a new life cycle that will set off freedom for you and generations to come.

The constellation method also recognizes three principles that support families in functioning well:

- **Inclusion rather than exclusion**. Everyone belongs to a family, whether alive or deceased, old or young, never born or presently living in the family.
- **Rank should be recognized**. In terms of influence, parents come before children, and grandparents come before parents. Previous marriages and significant relationships of parents should be acknowledged for the benefit of the children's health, for instance.
- **Unresolved trauma in past generations will affect future generations,** unless the trauma is appropriately acknowledged and addressed.

The second point, regarding the parents coming before children, resonated with me. Being the first generation born in America, you're often the one that goes first to college, and are probably fluent in English, with several advantages that, unfortunately, many of your family members don't share. Research shows that a vital wealth factor that contributes to specific ethnic groups not achieving wealth is that accumulated wealth often is shared with other family members who have not reached their goals. This latter group also has less access to technological advancements and to healthy habits. I live through that reality each day. It's like having two worlds that you have to balance: the progressive, open, expansive, and the one where you have to take care of parents and family members due to the disparity that exists between generations.

As a result, for several years, I placed my parents first. Without having children of my own, my parents have become my children, and the dynamics were simply unfulfilling to me, personally. In contrast, the way the family constellations approach displayed it, parents should support you as the child throughout your life. As a child, parents teach you their self-imposed values and discipline for your protection and care. However, as an adult, their role is not to be in front of you or to be your recipients (that's the placement of your children), or on your side (that's the placement of your partner).

When this pattern was explained to me, I was awed. It makes sense, but for many of us, our upbringing judges us for placing ourselves first. Since then, I've learned it's not a matter of not assisting your parents or helping others, but knowing that we each have a role and place, and there's a balance that needs to occur for our lives to fully achieve its potential, and to positioning ourselves as the sources and drivers of our lives. Without this placement, we experience emotions of fear, limitations, and unsettling directions.

Understanding the placement concept has helped me to communicate, to engage, and also to set accountability where it belongs. I'm no longer a child, so there's a level of engagement that has to occur with my parents. Maintaining this stance has helped remove the guilt associated with wanting to do things as expected, things often more appropriate towards a child. Acknowledging the root of your parent-child relationships helps you respect and be grateful for each role within a family, which is the first step in healing, followed by taking action, moving forward, and regaining control of your life.

Another fascinating insight I learned is that the relationship with your mother is reflected in the relationship you have with your organization or your business, if you're self-employed. As I shared in my childhood stories, my mother and I have not always seen eye-to-eye, regarding how I should look or my life's path. She often has ideals and a perception of who I should be, which don't necessarily align with my purpose. It's been difficult to recover from those moments, while still honoring and loving her. In parallel, my career has not always involved jobs that had the same pace or an organizational culture that aligned with my core values. Both examples resulted in disappointment and resentment towards essentially what was or is *feeding* you.

Consider that, from birth, our mother acts as the fountain of our life; from everything that flows over from her to us, we derive our existence. Where does our success begin? It begins with our mother. How does our success come to us? How can it happen? When our mother is welcome to come to us, and when we honor her as our mother. Focusing on not being right, instead of loving through respect and compassion, will continue hindering my relationship with my mother. Turning to others is a process that starts in our inner being, and it comes easily once we have successfully turned to our mother. This notion applies, regardless of whether or not your mother still lives.

Exercise:

1. We sit upright on the edge of a chair, and we breathe out deeply, through our mouth, and in through our nose. We keep our eyes open and repeat this breathing twice. Then we close our eyes and breathe normally. Our hands rest on our thighs with our palms turned upward.

2. Slowly we stretch our arms out in front of us, further and further, reaching out to someone. We remain sitting upright, sensing how our back becomes more upright as we reach out with our arms further and further. In our mind, we reach out to our mother.

3. Remaining in this position, we become aware of how many times and ways we have turned away from others, instead of turning towards them. We stay in this position, even if it is still difficult for us for the moment. We move our arms and our open hands forward even more, while still holding our back upright.

4. Slowly and gently, we open our eyes. Without moving, our eyes perceive our environment all at once, as a whole. We are turning to it, to the front, to each side, and even to the back.
5. We also turn our ears to our environment. We open them wide, ready and willing to hear everything and anything others want us to know, and together with them, we experience ourselves turned to our mother and to other people, in love and confidence, at one with them.
6. We take another three deep breaths. First, we breathe out, then we breathe in and out three times. We remain sitting upright, our back straight, slightly leaning forward.
7. Suddenly we feel a different connection with many people, our eyes wide open and shining, with our ears open to them, and we imagine ourselves turning to them differently, also to those we are connected with through our profession and our business.

What happens to our success now? Does it still keep us waiting? What happens to our joy and our happiness? They also turn to us, as our mother does.

It's important to acknowledge that our careers, business or job serves as a provider and an extension to our life's composition. Doing so helps us understand that we each have a role and a place. It fosters gratitude for who we are and are becoming. Ultimately, we come to terms with our respective placement in the world, and understand the impact our careers have on emotional well-being and overall alignment with our core values and life purpose.

Life Partners

In parallel, we may have our significant others, romantic partner, or spouse. In family constellations, they have a side-by-side placement next to us. It's like a united front toward a shared vision. Throughout my life, I hoped to find the right one. Well, it took several attempts, it seemed. But as I look at myself at each of those stages and periods, it has made sense. I attracted the same energy I manifested. Folks often say, when the least you expect, you find the "one." It's not about finding the one; it's beyond love. Instead, it's about how the two energies can fulfill a higher purpose.

I'm grateful for each of those relationships, they brought experience, and through those wounds eventually wholeness. Appreciation and gratitude are the beauty, joy, self-worth, truth, and love inside you, finding itself in another person. When we reverberate in deep appreciation, we experience our wholeness and oneness with all creation. When our heart fills with gratitude, we arrive fully in the present moment, letting go of our past regrets and concerns for the future. In this state of pure appreciation, we radiate the light of love to everyone we meet.

Osho became one of my favorite authors and spiritual experts when I read his book *Love*. The most important lesson I learned was that love is freedom. As most of us learned about love through our parents, our peers, and whatever exists in the outside world, and TV, for me, played a significant experience. Seven Disney movies had princesses marrying their soulmates with challenges in between and happily-ever-after endings. But love is well beyond a relationship or romantic encounter; it's how we connect first with ourselves and then with others. For years, I had to cleanse the lens of perception and see myself as we are: completely loved and completely lovable.

Despite what you may have been conditioned to believe, there is nothing that you have to do or reach to be worthy of love. Your true self is pure love, and you are already infinitely precious precisely as you are. This awareness of who you are connects you to your true self-esteem. This esteem is solid and unwavering. When you rest in your existence, you love yourself unconditionally. The approval rating of your ego, in contrast, is fickle and forever shifting. Your ego may approve of your performance one day, and then the next day, judge you as inadequate or lacking. As you practice meditation or silence, our awareness expands and awakens us to love.

Many people think of love as an emotion that comes and goes. In one moment, we feel intense passion, and in the next, we feel nothing at all. We may then become consumed by doubts about our relationships, or get caught up in an anxious search for love, striving to attract someone who will finally give us the love and approval we've longed for. But in truth, love isn't a capricious emotion, but a state of being. It is an experience of unity with all creation. In every moment, we can choose to be the presence of love and let that love guide all our words and actions. This choice will transform all of your relationships, including the one with yourself.

Looking back, my first marriage had a unique purpose. It ignited the notion that there was more to life than what tradition had taught me. As children, we know this, and then we become so involved with routine, and the immediate tasks of daily life become our primary drivers. Yet we know this from the moment we're born. When we're not listening, life gives us experiences. The scariest part is that life continues repeating itself until we finally get the lesson. Then our paths are clear to move on to the next phase.

Shortly after I divorced, I read Elizabeth Gilbert's famous memoir, *Eat, Pray, Love*. Coming from a very traditional family, the fact that I was divorcing brought embarrassment, and I experienced the inability to communicate to others about what I was going through. At least, it felt that way. I remember my mom kept my wedding pictures on her walls for years after the divorce. Most of the family's friends would ask, "When are you having babies?", thinking I was still married well after the daring event. So reading about another woman's experience – a rock bottom experience – gave me a sense of reality, knowing that other women and couples go through this. (Unfortunately, it's widely reported that divorce is a common experience.)

Also similar to Elizabeth's main character, I went on a journey of self-discovery. It was the first time I felt empowered to travel by myself, and I learned how much I enjoyed every aspect of it, but in particular, the food, the culture, and how others lived. All of a sudden, work demanded travel from me, and opportunities to travel opened up at every turn. I went to Italy on my own, and it was as magical as the book itself. I ate an entire margarita pizza for breakfast, all by myself, and it felt amazing.

It was just the beginning, and some of the cycles repeated themselves until I became genuinely available. Several years of similar unavailable relationships, of spiritual growth, and of friends that forever planted the seeds of love and kindness later, I met my now-husband. Without this path, I would've not been ready for him. He's one of the most pure-spirited people I know. He may disagree, but he does have the soul of a seven-year-old: he's transparent, and he's admitting of his downfalls. He brings me to life, because there are no masks between us. Whenever one of us attempts to put a mask on, or our egos are leading, there's discomfort, and our communication becomes less than fluent.

My first encounter with my husband, almost eight years ago, was not when we experienced the exciting fireworks. It wasn't until nearly four years ago that we started dating. To this date, we're both very grateful that the timing was right when it did happen. The love we had for our inner selves, eight years ago, was not ideal, and not the love we would have wanted for the other. My love was based on many expectations that I have outgrown since. In reality, I was looking for a partner to complete me. Who wants that? That means it's someone else's responsibility to make me happy. That's quite a risk and burden. As I mentioned earlier in the book, I was not available simply because I wasn't available to myself. This differs from a relationship that adds to your fulfillment, so that together, you're going to conquer your dreams. However, in a relationship, you remain individuals in addition to being a pair. You still have paths to walk, and your union becomes a manifestation of the universe's desire to reach a larger goal.

As I was writing this book, I was also planning a wedding. It's quite an exciting experience. We took the opportunity to learn about our communication styles, how we each process work, and how we prioritize. We used this work to bring out our authentic selves. As newlyweds, we have much to learn and natural barriers to confront as we progress through life. Because we're working toward a journey of living a human experience, we continue understanding how to demonstrate our life for each other. It's so important to know how we each receive and give love.

Love Languages

As we've learned, our Higher Power is the source of guidance and wisdom, which places us at the origin of our love and compassion. When united with a partner, the love expressed and shared becomes the source of your expansion as a couple. We have learned we love very differently. The way we give and receive love also changes over time. I invite you to learn about love languages. If you're familiar with this concept, it may be an opportunity to reassess. Gary Chapman's *Love Language* introduces the fascinating concept, as he describes it in his book, "We cannot rely on our native tongue if our spouse does not understand it. If we want them to feel the love we are trying to communicate, we must express it in our primary language." In his book, Chapman describes five love languages:

1. Words of affirmation
2. Quality of time
3. Receiving gifts
4. Acts of service
5. Physical touch

Chapman describes that by communicating love using your partner's style, you can fill their love tank.

Otherwise, your partner will feel unfilled, and the emotional love ties eventually will disintegrate.

Exercise: Take the <u>Love Language Quiz</u>. (See Appendix)

- What's your primary language?
- Were you surprised?
- If with a partner, what are his/her primary language? Were you surprised by each other's results?
- How much do you practice his/her language?
- How does he/she prioritize your primary love language?

When I first read the book, about ten years ago, I was all about the quality of time and physical touch. Similar to any concept that profiles you, we communicate with all, but lead with one language. One is not better than the other. Each language reflects preferences and tendencies. Your preferences are influenced by your understanding of your inner self, your external circumstances, and your relationship with love. Because love languages change with time, it's vital to ask your partner, friends, or others, "How do you feel loved?"

When you are on the same page about your love and the dynamics of giving and receiving, other areas that couples work through together like children, finances, career, and family obligations, become much simpler to address. On the other hand, not feeling loved creates a state of instability in relationships, often accompanied by indifference, resentment, and miscommunications. Back ten years ago, I was wounded, not enjoying my own company, so with any partner, spending time together was of the essence. Also, physical touch was how I expressed my love, and so I expected my partners to demonstrate it the same way. With an empty tank, most things about them would bother me.

Interestingly, today, much of that has changed. I'm super connected with my wants, but I'm also quite busy and a natural giver. So my tank fills through acts of service. I'm in an active stage of my life. With career and family obligations, I will welcome any break I can take. My husband leads with quality of time and physical touch, which is funny because that's how I used to communicate and to perceive love precisely. He's usually the event coordinator and schedules our outings. He's so much fun, and he likes to experience life through adventure. I have an opportunity to take the lead in scheduling time for us to explore, as I work at filling his tank. In this world of information, it is so easy to become distracted, thus giving him my undivided attention when he talks or even when we're watching TV is essential. I asked him what physical touch means to me, not assuming it's sexual. His answers extended to hugs and kisses and general touching throughout the day.

Throughout my life, I've experienced the balancing act of seeing romantic relationships as an obstacle or an asset to my career success, primarily because both required quality of time dedicated to it to see them grow. Since then, I've learned all areas of our lives require quality of time as we prioritize them, and they work in sync and influence each other. Over time, the amount of exerted effort may be less, because of the influence each area of your life has on the other. The opposite is also true. For example, the time in a meaningful relationship inspires growth and a purpose in us.

Research from Washington University in St. Louis by Jackson and Solomon even found that "a spouse's personality influences many daily factors that sum up and accumulate across time to afford one the many actions necessary to receive a promotion or a raise" (Everding, 2014, https://source.wustl.edu/2014/09/spouses-personality-influences-career-success-study-finds/). This means that, if you and your partner are on the same wavelength when it comes to professional paths, you will probably both succeed.

Communicating each other's goals as they evolve and surface is just as essential to sustaining a long-term relationship. I've been guilty of not communicating my plans effectively in the past, and it's work in progress. It's a matter of inclusivity. "The meeting of two personalities is like the contact of two chemical substances: if there is any reaction, both are transformed" (Jung, https://www.goodreads.com/quotes/23089-the-meeting-of-two-personalities-is-like-the-contact-of). Three paths have to align: the two individual tracks, and the one that you're forming as a couple. You must tackle the topic of your careers and pathways as a united front.

Exercise: Review and complete, independently or with your partner.

- What are your long-term professional goals? The answer to this question will shed light on what your partner has in mind for their career. It will be a great conversation starter as to what type of changes or priorities lie ahead. It's an opportunity to align your priorities and activities that you can invest time together to lift each other.

- What are your short-term professional goals? Understanding what motivates your partner about their current jobs will help you know short-term priorities. If they don't have something in mind, they may have a preference for how to better use their time.
- What's your one-, five-, and ten-year plan? It's essential to understand how you're each investing your time, discuss plans that perhaps impact the relationship, such as physical moves, purchasing homes, having children, and financial budgets.
- How do you plan to accomplish these professional goals? It's crucial that, as we evolve and think about how we achieve these goals, we identify the opportunity to reflect our own self-identity and also add value to the other person's professional plans.
- First, share what you want to do, and then ask what his/her thoughts are? Inclusion is key! I've learned that not only shows that you value your partner's opinion, but also that you're taking into consideration the closest person to you. This person is familiar with your strengths and opportunities, your tendencies, and persona, and they must be given the space to share their thoughts. It also promotes the notion of engagement as you plan for your future together.
- What have you accomplished in the last five years? Is it what you wanted to achieve?

Asking these questions opens the discussion to assess if he or she has focused on his or her dreams. It's an opportunity to rethink core values together and apart, and to formulate a shared vision that will set your relationship to a whole new level.

Friendships and Colleagues

It takes a village, they say. Over the years, I have been blessed to have met beautiful people who have come through my life. But I have also encountered friendships that had to be let go. Like many working adults, many of my best friends today have been or are co-workers. The concept of co-workers and interpersonal relationships will be forever a debated topic, as friendship often influences performance and productivity at work if there isn't a defined line or a high level of maturity between business and friendship.

According to a study on "Global Work Connectivity," over half of employees today feel lonely at work all or most of the time, and they also report a desire for more social interaction in the workplace. The study found that 60% of workers would be more inclined to stay with their employer if they had more friends at work. This does not mean that all your co-workers need to be your friends, nor can you only be productive by having friends. It becomes a conversation of synchronicity and attraction, further supporting the notion that having friendly relationships at work, can lead to:

- Higher job satisfaction levels: Having people that you spend so much time with that support and lift you will make your experience at work gain a more vibrant sense of achievement.
- Increased efficiency: When the team is in sync, and each member of the team is consciously bringing

their inner talents, gifts, and competencies, in combination with alignment and communication with others, it's a perfect recipe for performance.

- Ability to innovate: When you feel like your team and leadership has your back, it opens the space for creativity and exploration.
- Use friends as a support system: You feel empowered when other energies, support, and advocacy are shared.
- Improved communication skills: With stronger work relationships, like with any other, there's easy on engagement, relaying information, and the ability to productively process and facilitate action.

When you're connected to your source, and you find colleagues and friends who are aware that they have a more significant duty than their jobs, you know you've reached a whole new level. One day, I was having one of those (of many) tricky days at work. But the feeling was well beyond work itself; it was life and its burdens that were bringing me down. My office neighbor and her best friend came by to say hi. We know each other so well, that by glancing at each other, we know what's going on in each other's worlds. Then, in February 2018, one of them anointed me with the power of the source, by rubbing oil on my feet, similar to when Jesus was anointed with costly oil by Bethany in the Bible.

Now, I look back and say to myself as I laugh, "The things I've done at work!" But the universe sends you its troopers and lightworkers, to make sure you're being nourished and cared for, as you're embarking on this new journey. You may feel you cannot do this alone, but you aren't alone if you have an intimate decision with your Higher Power. More importantly, you dedicate time to having conversations, not just when you need it the most, but just as you have them with coworkers, your partner or best friend. To this date, I cannot thank these two coworkers enough; they are my best friends and sisters, sent to me from a place of love.

Exercise: Respond to the following questions:

- How do you prioritize friendships outside and inside the workplace?
- Do you invest time in forming meaningful relationships?
- Now that you understand how vital workplace friends are, how might you go about developing these critical relationships, if you don't already have them?
- What if you're new to the job and don't know many people?
- How do you reach out and start to build some meaningful workplace friendships?

One of my wise friends at work once told me: "Receive from the person that can give you." By keeping this thought in mind, I started seeing friendships in light of a support system, or family. Let's face it; many of us spend more time with colleagues than with our families. Even if you have families, their inner selves may not be available to you. I carry that message very carefully with me. I often had an expectation about what my mom, my sister, or close relatives would give me, because they were associated with me through blood. Who else can be closer? My reality has been one of which friendships have encouraged me to prioritize, appreciate, and respect each person for who they indeed are. Friendships, similar to romantic partners, are a source of knowledge, support, and enhance the connectivity we each bring to the universe.

In preceding chapters, we discussed assessments that look at talents, strengths, even how the worlds sees you, through Hogshead's Fascination Advantages Profile. Take the opportunity to make a conscious investment in learning more about your colleagues at work, regardless of your friendship. By understanding your areas of strength and opportunities, you're opening the doors for increased engagement, use of resources in the workplace, and communication. Ultimately, we will be contributing to ourselves by seeing the light in others. The company you work for will also benefit from enhanced productivity and efficiency. Lastly, and very importantly, you will be lifting and inspiring someone else. The cycle of fascinating, encouraging, and empowering others becomes our mission when we see the power of relationships in and outside of the workplace.

Pets

Let's not forget our loyal companions at home – yes, pets! Personally, ever since I was a child, I was inclined toward them. I remember living in the Dominican Republic and owning seventeen different pets at once. I shared with you how much easier it was to communicate with them while growing up. They are so nurturing and pure, which replicates the light of a child. Although they may not have the intellect of humans, they very much have their purposes. The same happens with plants and other living creatures. Unlike humans, they follow their continuous cycle of life, consistently.

Today, my husband and I own a dog that bursts with energy and grace. We adopted her from a shelter two years ago, and I genuinely feel she's playing a role and purpose in our family. She arrived amid a significant family health concern, and since then has been a companion to me beyond what words can explain. As in any relationship, she has needs and preferences. If we were to asses, "filling her tank" mostly involves treats and belly rubs! That might be the case for many pups out there, but for us, she's certainly one of a kind.

We joke that she portrays a human personality; her expressions and maneuvers often align with that of her owners. Any dog owner can tell you how receptive pets are to their owners' emotions. They may be limited in language, but they are seriously intuitive. More and more, haven't we seen pets being allowed to come work? Big names like Google, Mashable, and Amazon have pet-friendly policies that welcome non-assistive companions into the office daily. The benefits are touted widely: pets help reduce stress and may increase communication and socialization, and there is no shortage of research to this effect. According to one <u>study</u> (See Appendix) that surveyed thirty-one companies in Kentucky, pets in the workplace allow owners to express a bit of their personality (Wells and Perrine, 2001).

When polled about the benefits of pets in the office, participants (n=97 cat owners; n=110 dog owners) reported:

- pets relieved stress (cats 29 %; dogs 21 %)
- made the office more friendly (cats 21 %; dogs 18%)
- provides a positive diversion (cats19%; dogs 9%)

Inarguably, pets can be loving companions, both at home and at work. The bottom line: take the opportunity to connect with living creatures, because they, too, carry wisdom, whether it is through the way they communicate or even through their furry paws.

We have learned the power of relationships, more importantly, the fact that we each have a way that we can contribute. Acknowledging our roles and the differences we bring, each of us serves as a conduit of love, respect, and compassion. Each individual carries a unique power. Don't take for granted differences in communication, competencies, talents, and even blind spots; instead remember to look at yourself first, appreciate the knowledge and support that our families, friends, and colleagues bring to our lives, and be aware that we're connected to achieve something more significant. It becomes our mission to work with the village both given to us and that we embrace over time. What's the best gift we can leave future generations? Our own kids? A world that has genuine people, who have found their position in the world, who do not look to the sides for comfort, but inward. Then the power of the masses really kicks off. Generations will benefit from meaningful love, and people that will act as the greatest support system of all. The wars, violence, and greed that have plagued the world will be lessened when individual growth is embraced, and we respect others for being themselves. Only in those moments will we see our purpose and love for each other.

Chapter 11:
Step 7 – Contribution and Community: The Power of Your Talents and Gifts

"Hide not your talents, they for use were made,
What's a sundial in the shade?"
– Benjamin Franklin

This chapter will help you understand how giving and sharing your talents and gifts increases the flow of abundance and fulfillment in your career and wealth.

Big or Small, It Counts

"The moment you become miserly you are closed to
the basic phenomenon of life: expansion, sharing.
The moment you start clinging to things, you have
missed the target – you have missed. Because things are
not the target, you, your innermost being,
is the target – not a beautiful house, but a beautiful you;
not much money, but a rich you; not many things,
but an open being, available to
millions of things."
– Osho

If you recall from previous chapters, we touched upon giving and sharing as a method of personal growth and self-management. As you evolve into your universe called "role", you'll realize there's an urgent need to share, give, and expand. It happens naturally, something we often add to our plans; but honestly, it's one of the first changes you'll see as you deep-dive into self-work. There are so many joys in life, and I must say one of the most gratifying, long-lasting impressions one can make is sharing your gifts and talents. It's a feeling and a behavior that come in one piece. From the beginning of time, I would see my parents giving their time and sharing at every opportunity. I'm grateful for their deeds, as it became contagious and a behavior that has given so much in return.

Folks ask me, "What do I have to share? I don't have enough to share", or "I don't have the money to share." Giving comes in different flavors and approaches. The first step is understanding the value of giving. Similar to gratitude, it multiplies your presence, your strengths, and your resources when you're a position of understanding how you can contribute to your life. Your presence alone is a contribution, and the more you live in your core values, in gratitude, and using inner wisdom to guide your steps, the more impact and fulfillment your act of giving has.

Giving Using Your Love Language

Sharing your gifts and talents generally comes in forms of time, functions, or effort and monetary contributions. Remember: The act of giving comes from a source of love. Love is an action; it carries movement and energy. We often describe it as a feeling, but it's not. It is action itself. The configuration of the action, like the people involved, and our thoughts, bring us the feeling, but it starts with an action. You may provide at your job, within a community, or through a charitable organization. You can provide your abilities as you run errands. Don't forget that your talents are at their highest with mastery. Giving takes a lot less effort than most think. You'll reap the rewards of so many opportunities, both for yourself and others.

Start by giving according to your primary love language. This means, you can give your talents and gift as an act of service, for example, serving food to homeless shelter during Thanksgiving, giving quality time to mentor children, or adults in your industry or field. Or give a tangible gift, such as monetary or material goods, or words of affirmation that compliments someone at the store for their fantastic customer service. Or offer physical touch, like volunteering at a local hospital to rock babies in the NICU, or to greet elders at a nursing home.

Exercise: List your love languages in ranking order, using your Love Language report results. Next to each, list the opportunities you have to give the hard and soft talents you identified in earlier chapters, for example, computer skills (hard) to compassionate (soft).

So Why Is It So Important to Give Your Talents?

Skills have the highest contribution when in sync with others. Each person comes with their own set of strengths, gifts, and abilities. Together they meet the highest level of the universe's objectives. And the more you give, the more you receive. If you think from a place of limitation, your mind will tell you that you don't have sufficient time, money, and talents, so what exactly are you going to give, right? Well, even if you think those things, giving is more like hitting the Staples "That Was Easy" button. It initiates the cycle of abundance, and similar to gratitude, the areas you contribute to the most will be areas where you'll never lack. If you think from a place of abundance, you already know you're never going to run out of talent. Talent gets better with mastery, so it's in your best interest to prioritize this aspect of your career development journey.

Gifts benefit others and change lives. Because the art of giving is universal, you can lift yourself and others. Others who are providing to you are also enabling you to be more successful. Because giving is a cycle, when you enhance others' ability to become successful, the universe, through your Higher Power, will make sure the right resources are there, and the doors are wide open for you, too. We may take it for granted, but we feed on others' talents every day. We benefit from Steve Job's Apple creations, Edison's light bulb, Ford's automotive ideas, or our mom's cooking. We often notice Saint Mother Teresa's level of giving, but she had a unique set of talents and made it her mission to share. What we do share in common with her, however, are the hours of the day. We can find a way to contribute. Big and small are subject to interpretation and often an "ego" term to use. Contributions bring us together, and that's all you need to know. Finding a place and time for our priorities not only positions us to rise to the occasion, but to enhance our natural gifts, and to see for ourselves the magnitude of empowerment and riches it brings to our life.

For the last three years, I've been working with the Bowery Mission, which is a faith-based organization that works with diverse portfolios for services (including homeless, children and youth programs, women's shelter, food access) among several charitable and community services. I volunteer my time and talents to work with the children of Mont Lawn City Camp, which is a leadership program that serves children in underserved areas of our community. I love my children. It's nuts for me to get up on a Saturday morning, after an excruciating week at work. Absolutely. But I know how I'm going to feel after hanging out with my fellow mentors and all the kids that join us. It's addicting to feel good.

The kids consider City Camp their second home, and they feel safe and part of a place that accepts them as they are. Growing up, I didn't think that I belonged. My parents and family gave me as much love as they knew, and the way they knew to give love. But I, too, similar to these children, came from communities often not exposed to what else is out there in the world. All of us have an opportunity to have this exposure, regardless of our community demographics. If you can be part of the change, how amazing would that be? You can be, precisely the way you are, and sometimes with simply lifting a finger. For example, through my work, I met the founder of an organization that originated from his struggles navigating the healthcare system in his attempts to help his aunt manage her health. Today, he's doing greatness to connect people in need of resources, such as food, shelter, and social services with organizations in the community. He continues expanding his business model to partner with others that are doing greatness.

Another example is *Give to a Neighbor*, which allows you to give material goods to neighbors in your area who need a specific product. How often do you place an Amazon order as you walk your dog, or even when you're talking on the phone? I do it all the time, in case you were wondering. You can give with the same ease. Talking of Amazon, did you know you can also contribute to charities as you order through Amazon? By simply changing the URL used to login to your Amazon account, through smile.amazon.com, you are positioned to donate items to the charity organizations of your choice. No additional costs to you. You spend money on Amazon, and you automatically are contributing. Amazing, isn't it? Find your way, embrace, and share.

You also will be happier by giving. Doing more of what you do awesomely already can only bring joy. Gallup (2016) conducted a research study on people who use their strengths every day and how it affects their performance and, overall, their quality of life. Gallup found out that people who use their strengths and talents (something that comes naturally and can be enhanced through practice) every day are six times more likely to be engaged on the job.

The key points from their findings: People using their assets experienced:

1. Improved health and wellness,
2. Less worry, stress, anger, sadness, or physical pain,

3. A to boost their positive emotions,
4. More energy to face the day, and
5. Higher levels of engagement in a task.

Gallup's data also show that only learning their strengths alone makes employees 7.8% more productive, while teams that focus on strengths every day have 12.5% greater productivity.

In working with my teams, I've made it a priority to shift from supporting functional areas to using people's strengths and placing them in areas where 65% of the time their work is driven off their strength, and 35% of the time is push and areas of opportunities. This will enable them to not only seek growth in the right areas, but to master areas of strength and be motivated enough to overcome the barriers and strain that working on opportunities can bring to one's career. And if you're in the process of transitioning to another job or career, you must bring your strengths to the forefront.

So, *leave a legacy*. I'm often asked, "How would you like to be remembered by future generations?" My answer is simple. I don't need to be recognized or remembered as Vanessa, who did whatever. I want to leave a footprint that's embedded in people's way of living their lives, their authentic perspective of the world, so that so many of us share our talents as our authentic selves, it becomes a seamless act of love and not something to remember. Do we remember Edison each day when we turn on our lights? No. But his work has transcended generations and has set the foundation for others to follow. I've always had it in my heart to impact the masses. Seeing the talents in others and empowering others at each opportunity, I believe that you, too, can leave a legacy;

the magic lies in the changes we're unable to see. I trust that your talent is that powerful.

And, *make money*. As we discussed in the chapter of wealth and setting financial goals, it's essential that we establish a relationship with money and set goals. After all, we need money to live stable lives, and to secure basic needs like food and shelter.

The highest performing individuals that I've worked with understand and orchestrate their talents daily. It also helps to be in an environment that fosters such ability. Reinforce the importance of understanding not only an organization's opportunities, but the culture and values of the organization, as you would with any relationship. Yes, you and your organization have a relationship like any other. It calls for management, respect, wisdom, and authenticity. The mutual love language needs to be in alignment with your career priorities for both parties to reach fulfillment, meaning high performance (organizational expectation) and job satisfaction (individual expectation).

Exercise: Ask yourself these questions:

- What traits and actions bring fulfillment to you through your organization?
- What can be different in your organization or future job?
- What contributions do you feel your organization or role brings to you today?
- What things can you do differently at your organization or next job?

Identify and document these areas of opportunity. Remember: Regardless of your path, newly learned behavior and recently identified skills and talents must be positioned appropriately to develop and to be used more fully.

We must find ways to use our talents regardless of whether we're considering working in the same or a different field. We often overthink how skills are used, and if they match with what we're doing and our job. The reality is that talent sharing is much more fundamental than a job. Remember: It's who you want to be, versus what you want to do. Gallup's news article "How Employees' Strengths Make Your Company Stronger" (2016) cited ways to use those talents. Whether we are excellent in doing calligraphy, tinkering, drawing, or anything else, there is always an opportunity waiting for us.

Personal development is at the core. Practicing and feeling accomplished as you give and share your talents enhances mastery, but also advances growth in your field. For example, I work in healthcare, and in my role, I can be involved in data, reporting, financial modeling, networking, and community work, to mention a few tasks. Because I'm involved in such an array of functions where I can contribute my talents of progressive work and innovation, I can choose the areas that I love to do best and focus on those. I have also found new skills that I didn't know I had, or positioned myself to help in ways I was able to, like community empowerment.

You see, when you are good at something, and you obsess about it, you become the asset. You have leverage and can add value in areas that are unique to you. We discussed how you're the asset in our first chapter. Giving is the opportunity to share yourself as an asset.

Be grateful. Your talents are given to you and only you. You may say, well, others are good at painting, writing, or being a leader. Of course, that might be true, but you were born differently, your DNA is different, and no two people are configured in the same way. You look the way you look and walk the way you walk because it fits everything else you will do in life. Your talents and gifts were given as the tool to get there.

"Your talent is God's gift to you. What you do with it is your gift back to God."
– Leo Buscaglia

Start with gratitude. Whomever you consider your Higher Power and source of your creation, be thankful. Gratitude is fundamental to every area of our lives. It promotes fulfillment, strength, empowerment, courage, compassion, and transmits the love we need to be authentic to ourselves and others. By doing so, you'll be promoting the cycle of talent sharing and initiating a process of abundance, a world where we will not lack anything because we're each contributing and performing the part that we were intended to.

Power in the multitudes is the reason we assemble. There is power in numbers and in the masses. On January 2, 2019, I remember turning on the radio station; it was my first day back to work from a holiday, and I needed inspiration. I found a radio station, called K-LOVE, and the hosts, Skip and Amy, were promoting a thirty-day positivity challenge. I'm, like, "Sure, why not?" The challenge was to listen to their station for thirty consecutive days. The station is well beyond the music; it's about the energy and words that it carries. There hasn't been a single day that there wasn't a song, topic of discussion, or message that I needed to hear at that moment. The station is funded through donations, and one day they were asking for donations. It was impressive the number of people who called in, stating the power this station has in their lives.

This story serves as a confirmation that people have life circumstances like yours, often worse that what you've ever experienced. It's also a reminder that you are blessed. There's power from all sources, even a radio station, as long as it speaks to you. Since then, I, too, donate. There are hundreds of thousands of people listening and sending each other happy and loving thoughts each day. Masses don't have to be in one physical place; we just have to exist and to know that we are out there in order to support each other.

In *Wealth for All: Living a Life of Success at the Edge of Your Ability* (2016), Idowu Koyenikan says, "There is immense power when a group of people with similar interests gets together to work toward the same goals." We first become ourselves, then all aspects of our lives become one. You are your relationships, your wealth, your career, your talents. You will attract people that are not necessarily similar to you, but like you, are in a position of giving, whatever skills and method they use is irrelevant. Together you are contributors to humanity's mission and a higher purpose. You will inspire each other and maybe get lost in a hiking trail. Yes, that happened to me, and I am grateful.

Healing is part of empowerment.

"We don't heal in isolation, but in community."
– S. Kelley Harrell

I have several communities that, in my lifetime, I know I will go back to in order to share. I have my industry, and I have pockets of NYC, and then I have my friends and family as a community – the same people who have been my biggest supporters and share tremendous love and joy; and there's also the community of the Dominican Republic. The act of giving and sharing is and will evolve to be different for each one. You see, when you're connected with yourself, your inner child, Higher Power, and wisdom, you're able to transcend, through the power of giving, into the generations and into pockets of community. Your world becomes so expansive and present, that whatever is in front of you is seen as an opportunity; you will see and surrender to the job you were created to perform at the right moment and the right place.

Giving and sharing your talents is an act of love. It brings not only benefits to yourself, but to others and to the universe, towards a greater mission that you may not understand today. It positions you to enhance your personal development, but instantly you create a cycle of growth and abundance. Knowing that you have gifts to give, and that you only really need yourself to do so, makes it accessible to us all with little change in where we are today. Remember: Change starts with one person, but healing becomes a community affair. The more we use our talents, and become masters, the more opportunities will come our way. Be grateful for exactly how you were designed and created. Develop a SMART goal to identify ways to contribute and share your talents and strengths as part of your career or any aspect of your life.

Chapter 12:
Step 8 – Health and Wellness: Preparing Your Body, Mind, and Spirit for Your Next Move

"The secret of health for both mind and body is not to mourn for the past, not to worry about the future, or not to anticipate troubles, but to live in the present moment wisely and earnestly."
– Buddha

In this chapter, you will learn how to read and nourish your body, so that you are ready to transition into her new job and phase in your life, and feel confident about job security.

In *The Book of Secrets: Unlocking the Hidden Dimensions of Your Life* (2005), Deepak Chopra beautifully explains, "If you obsess over whether you are making the right decision, you are basically assuming that the universe will reward you for one thing and punish you for another. Every significant vital sign – body temperature, heart rate, oxygen consumption, hormone level, brain activity, and so on – alters the moment you decide to do anything ... decisions are signals telling your body, mind, and environment to move in a certain direction."

Our bodies are indeed a work of art. When we think about their daily functions, we can only be grateful for our health. Even if we're going through times of sickness or fatigue, at some point, the body was healthy, and we must be grateful for those times. When people say, "I'm in tune with my body", what are they really saying? It might tell them when it needs something, or when something is "off." Our bodies serve as a barometer of our overall wellness, but they also protect and respond to our emotions. The body is your physical profile. It represents you in a human state.

For many years, well into my young adult life, particular body features bothered me. Was I tall enough, was my hair the right length and texture, was I too thin or too big? Did my legs match the rest of the body? Was my behind the right shape? Was my nose too wide? Then I'd watch TV and run through comparisons of the things that could be different. We started this book by reviewing how you're the most valuable asset. Your creation has a unique purpose. And as you continue working on personal growth and self-evaluation, you'll notice how your ability to produce and share becomes more and more dependent on your overall health.

Just today, as I was meeting with my boss, he graciously told me, "You look like crap." I have a terrible cold, and haven't carved out time to visit the doctor. I probably should have rested more, too. Even during the most exciting of times, like writing a book or working at the job of your dreams, you must listen to your body – sometimes you need to slow down, or it's nudging you to treat it with more love. Regardless, maintaining a healthy mind, body, and spirit is your main priority. Without that, you're unable to efficiently and productively share your talents or manifest the energy of your authenticity.

Healthy habits start with you, your family, and home, and over time, become part of your natural progression of transformation. As with any transition, like a career transition or change in job, your immune system is under stress. Our bodies respond in their attempts to protect us from any pain and impact from changes. You're much more prone to an autoimmune response, too, and so it's essential to keep in the body in its optimal state. If you don't already have a routine or real understanding of what works for your body, you will now.

Dosha: Discovering Your Mind-Body Type

Did you ever wonder why you feel cold all the time versus your partner who is always warm? Or why your body has always been a certain way, but now you're having new reactions or things are not sitting well? According to the Indian medical system of Ayurveda (which translates to "knowledge of life"), a system of healing that examines physical constitution, emotional nature, and spiritual outlook in the context of the universe, a universal life force manifests as three different energies, or doshas: Vata, Pitta, and Kapha. We're all made up of a unique combination of these three forces. As you move through life, the proportion of each of the three doshas continually fluctuates. According to your environment, your diet, the seasons, the climate, your age, and many other factors. As they move into and out of balance, the doshas can affect your health, energy level, and general mood. Mostly, by understanding our natural mind-body compositions, we're able to nourish and support it the way it's most appropriate for its type.

Characteristics of Three Doshas

- *Vata Dosha:* Slender with prominent features, moody, impulsive, enthusiastic. This dosha is associated with the large intestine, pelvis, bones, ears, thighs, and skin.
- *Pitta Dosha:* Medium build, well-proportioned, stable weight. This dosha is associated with the small intestine, stomach, sweat glands, eyes, skin, and blood.
- *Kapha Dosha:* Solid, heavy, reliable, with a tendency to be overweight. This dosha is associated with the lungs, chest, and spinal fluid.

Exercise: Many resources are available on Ayurveda. Take the dosha quiz (https://shop.chopra.com/dosha-quiz/) to find your dominant dosha. Our composition includes all three, but usually, one or two are dominants. By aligning our dosha to our lifestyles, diet, and health routine, we can achieve maximum health and mental balance. Here are my results:

Vata: 80
Pitta: 10
Kapha:10

According to Chopra's site, the results indicate, "Since Vata is the principle of movement and change, you will tend to always be on the go, with an energetic and creative mind." Sounds just like me! Similar to our energy profile exploring the inner to physical composition of our body, dosha provides us the mind-to-body composition. Combined, we have the full dimensions of our natural selves.

You can continue exploring the <u>Chopra Center website</u> (See Appendix) to learn more about what diets, meditation, aromatherapy, stress-relieving activities, and a host of tools that will help you retain your balance. We are often trying to work against or opposite our natural state, especially when it comes to the physical body. Or we want to be or feel like others do. When we work against our natural tendencies, it leads to imbalances, decreased productivity, and, therefore, fulfillment and performance.

Exercise: Refer to the Chopra Center website to identify what characteristics balance your dosha, and create (or modify) a plan using SMART goals to integrate into your lifestyle.

Diet and Exercise

In my twenties, I was "anti-work out", because I was so young and influential. Ha! As you pile life on top of you, you realize that your body is only able to sustain so much. The most significant shift I've noticed in recent years is my energy level. As a Vata, when I'm balanced, I'm bursting with energy, engaging, creative. On less than optimum days, my perspective changes, I see people in a different light and often want to sleep. I have tried several workouts from kickboxing, biking, aerobics, and when I read about my dosha, yoga and Pilates seem like a more natural fit. Because Vatas tend to be more on the go, and our composition is air and space, it makes sense that more grounded activities create a better flow to balance our energy.

The Power of Water

Constant, on-the-go motion required hydration. You guessed it: drink water! I remember watching Cameron Diaz one day, chugging a liter of water on the Dr. Oz show, probably over three years ago. The actress swore it had changed her life and helped kick start her day. Of course, I tried it. For many years, I would avoid drinking water to minimize having to use the restroom. After all, work was so important, and each meeting had to take priority over my bladder. I look back at this behavior and wonder if I was utterly out of my mind. Since then I've consistently made it a point to wake up to water first thing in the morning.

When you start with the right decision in the morning, to nourish and give your body life, that sets an entire day of healthy patterns. I now drink about fifty-five ounces of water per day, which works well for my body weight and recommended daily intake. Physically, it has helped me improve the overall feeling and appearance of my skin. I'm a long sufferer of the scars and itches of eczema. Also, my body does not retain water. I didn't know it did until I started drinking water and noticed my weight was no longer fluctuating like it did. Emotionally, I feel more alert and focused in the morning and throughout the day. Coffee drinkers may argue against this, but really, if you have water and good spirits, you'll get a double dose of natural caffeine.

Whole 30

Your diet is a reflection of your ability to nourish your most important asset. It's a conduit to a basic, but critical survival mechanism. Imagine fueling your car with the appropriate fuel and oil, designed specifically for your car to maximize its performance. The same applies to your body and your performance at work. Identifying nutrients that are whole and compatible with your body determines your mental and physical capacity. A game-changer for me was learning about the Whole 30. About a year ago, my husband came back from a CrossFit class and asked me what I thought about doing the Whole 30, as part of a challenge he wanted to enroll in. I remember saying, "Sure, how bad can it be?" After all, we'd only be giving up primarily alcohol and sugar. I'm not even into sweets, I thought.

The diet encourages eating real food and eliminating others, like sugar, grains, dairy, legumes, MSG, and junk food/treats. One of the hardest realities for me was looking through most food labels and learning that sugar is in pretty much everything we'd buy, that wasn't vegetable or protein. *Have we steered away so much from real food that our source of energy comes from caffeine and sugar?* These were my thoughts as I ate cauliflower for the third time that week. Things started getting hairy by the end of the second week, when I was tired of having to prepare and cook meals for fourteen consecutive days. Most of our meals weren't all that different from the norm, but not having pizza and lazy Monday Thai was a downer for me. Eating out was a challenge. It was easier to know what ingredients you consume at home; and going out was a bourbon temptation. I also craved sweets after dinner, which I occasionally would have with my husband after dinner, but not often.

Depriving my body of sugar created a little cookie monster of me. I lost about three pounds in the process. We completed thirty days (well, I rounded to twenty-seven). But, wow! What an accomplishment! Your body comes out almost having a different taste palate. First, I now feel boozie with only one drink. Ever since, I rarely want to drink alcohol; instead, it's a social affair, if that. I also learned that sugar is my enemy. Since the minute I was born, I've had chronic eczema. I learned that stress and sugar make my skin angry at me. Sugar also causes extreme fatigue and even a state of craving other, less healthy options. It's no surprise, because we attract who we are. Beans, which I love, were also no good for me, and I have reduced my intake, which aligns with the nutritional guidelines of Vata as well. In addition, I had **no** digestive issues during this period. It's not like this change rocked my world, but some people describe feeling like a different person after 30 days. For me, I became more in tune with my body; plus there are some ingredients that I have not reintroduced into our diet whenever possible, like sugar and soy.

Successful and long-lasting behavior when it comes to nutrition is to do what works best for you and one that speaks the language of your body. I think Whole 30 was a great experience, and I came out learning so much and also amazing recipes, that otherwise, I would not have tried. But like anything else in life, balance, and appreciation for one's natural state are most important.

Exercise: Through my recipe seeking journey, I found Lisa Bryan, author of the Downshiftology website (See Appendix), who's a passionate food expert. If you'd like, visit her website, which contains a wealth of knowledge and tips on everything from food by diet to lifestyle. I encourage your spouse or friends also to be part of any diet and exercise journey, especially if you're trying a method for the first time. Learning to leverage our relationships through any change or transformation is empowering, and increases your commitment to achieve higher targets, because positive intent and encouragement are coming your way.

Listening to Your Body

Tuning in to your body sometimes requires you to drop flat on the ground, rather than aggravate allergic reactions. On three occasions, this has happened to me throughout my lifetime, usually, during very stressful times, two of them associated with career decisions or transitions. Doctors cannot diagnose or share what precisely the cause is, but indeed each of those scenarios was an attempt from the universe for me to slow down. Third time's a charm? Well, I wouldn't call it charm, but you do indeed start reading the symptoms much earlier before the actual event takes place. I've also experienced allergy attacks and facial swelling. These are examples of red flags. For me, these flags meant, "Vanessa, rest." That simple.

My nature is dynamic, on the go, with lots of movement. My body needs rest. All of us need rest, but in particular, because of my usual high energy and motivation, it's easy for me to slip when it comes to having downtime. Going to sleep earlier, for example – for me, this often means I'm the couch laying on top of my husband and the dog laying on top of me, but still, it happens. Finding quiet, whether it's in the morning or end of day, is now part of my daily routine. It's when you're experiencing symptoms that are extreme or just never experienced before, that you should seek medical care. From my experience, there's a much bigger message behind these scenarios.

Exercise: We learned about chakras and how they influences the flow of energy throughout our bodies. Now, try to recall a moment when you may have experienced one of the worst headaches, or maybe abdominal pain? Perhaps an intense back pain or tense shoulders? What was happening during this time? Did you (or do you) need a rest day, or maybe a month?

If you're trying to think about the last time you took a vacation or a sick day, schedule time off now. Mental health is real. You shouldn't wait until you're sick, need to run an errand, or flying out of the country to plan time off. Just being home on a Friday afternoon with no agenda may be all that you need. Many of us, especially when transitioning, are either extra busy tying loose ends or preparing for the world ahead. Regardless of your stage, you must give yourself time to create mental capacity between career stages, to increase space for creativity and the newness that lies ahead.

Listening to your body starts by understanding what's normal or usual behavior. You must first identify what is normal and reasonable, in order to locate a body trigger or when it's talking to you. Let's walk through a few scenarios to watch out during any transition, but those most commonly experienced during a career shift.

First, are you burnt out? Fatigued or in low energy? Experiencing sudden change in perspective, foggy mind, lack of concentration, or low motivation? Little things that wouldn't faze you are annoying the poop of you. "Yes", you might say, "I experience digestive issues." It sounds like stress to me. Burnout is a result of extreme focus and an unmet need to regain balance. Take a look at your wheel of life and see where there's an opportunity to shift. Exercise, a healthy diet, meditation, rest, and sleep will help, but ultimately, addressing and reprioritizing the culprit of the imbalance guarantees sustainable change. If the cause is the job you're about to leave, well, there you have it. But ensure you have a way of *maintaining* your body and mental health, so you carry healthy behaviors into your shiny role. Let's learn from prior experience and implement.

Next, are you moody? If you seem anxious or in a funk, it's essential to understand why and where the feelings are coming from. Especially if it lingers, or if there's a pattern of when you feel a certain way, it's essential to address these moods. Make sure to feel them, acknowledge, and address. Don't settle for feelings feeling of anger, depression, or fear. Use your relationships or seek professional help, as appropriate. *You* choose how you feel each day.

Or, are you noticing appetite changes? This is a big one for me. During seasons of hyper-focus (I swing between foggy and hyperactivity, depending on my environment and stress levels), my appetite tends to take a toll. Shifts in appetite might be related to emotional or environmental changes. Was it a particular food that triggered it? As you recall, I learned how angry sugar made my skin. Do a sanity check by journaling your food intake and frequency. It's inexpensive, and additionally, you can do a process of elimination to identify foods that simply no longer serve you.

Muscle soreness is also a biggy. When I first started practicing yoga and Pilates, I attributed a lot of aches to the workout. Your body tenses to protect you all day long in areas you may not be aware of. Keep those in mind. My trigger areas are the lower and mid-back and shoulders. That's where I retain my stress and crunch up, although I miss those cues throughout the day. Try a massage and ask your massage practitioner if any specific areas seem more prone to knots or tension. He or she may give you guidance on how to identify when the pressure is coming, and how to prevent it in the future. Muscle soreness has a "closing" effect on your body. When your body is tense, energy and circulation don't flow as they should, depriving the organism of its natural frequency, oxygen, and even nutrients.

Finally, is it sleep, or, better said, the lack of? What are your natural sleeping habits? At what time do you go to sleep? Do you usually wake up in the middle of the night? Do you have trouble going to sleep? Are you waking up earlier than usual? Your mind might be at a higher pitch than usual all day; however, it's essential that your body is at rest, and sleeping at least seven hours. Take a look at other aspects, like keeping your room at cooler temperatures, disconnecting from devices at least two hours before bedtime, running a fan or using a sound machine, and watch for your dinner schedule and other stressful triggers that might be keeping you up at night.

Body reactions are quite telling in my life. Anything from an upset stomach, to skin or allergy reactions. We develop new triggers with age, as your body changes.

Your body is probably at a state of high alert, and might be sensitive to things like gluten or lactose, or allergic to pollen. Seek attention from a doctor so that he/she can identify the trigger, so you can avoid or manage it.

Trust your judgment. Your inner guidance will never fail. The more you're connected with yourself, the more you'll understand your triggers, what a good versus lousy day means. Is it just soreness from your workout, or tension you're holding onto? You'll receive the answer.

Body-Mind-Spirit Balancing

As we've learned, the mind and body are always connected; your spirit is the energy that brings the body to life. Our chakras are connected to our psyche as well as to physical symptoms. As you learn to listen to your body, and to make the connections to other factors that may be influencing your career decisions and overall well-being, each symptom becomes a sign of potential acknowledgment or change.

After my divorce, I developed a long-lasting series of yeast infections. For my female readers, you can appreciate what I'm about to say. You don't want to make "it" angry. Mine was bitter all the time, and had many triggers, for example, going swimming or going to the gym, wearing the wrong underwear. I tried an array of homeopathic treatments, which only worked temporarily. In my search for a cure, I learned that I had to look beyond the end point, which was the infection itself. One must look at the life state as a whole. At the root of it all, the issue was related to the external needs and wants that made me feel secure. Shifting to chakra talk, the source of the problem emanated from the root and solar plexus chakras. It was the time of unavailable partners in my life, and it was clear that if I didn't solve the bigger problem, the yeast infection was there to stay. It was also a time when I did not prioritize my body, which we learned is our most valuable asset. This resulted in dozens of treatments not working long term.

Once I removed toxic relationships and emotional attachments that no longer served me, suddenly I went three weeks with no yeast infection, then it was two months, then six. Haven't had another yeast infection since. Recognizing early and even later signs of body changes, and what they are building to, is a good start toward your inner-to-outer body language bond. The same applied to my career and role at work. For about four years, I would consistently suffer from laryngitis, losing my voice as a result of common colds. But it went beyond that. It was a reflection of needing to find and use my work to establish my role. Also, it was connected to being comfortable engaging and using my resources to enable change in the complex work of healthcare. Balancing chakras is about assessing all life components and identifying triggers. You will see resolution of symptoms as you address triggers.

Exercise: The next few paragraphs contain a description of common symptoms experienced when chakras are unbalanced, and should always be used in conjunction with medical guidance, as appropriate. As you walk through each step in your career plan, consider performing a body scan (See Appendix), to identify triggers and discomforts. Other common ways of balancing your chakras, include, yoga, meditation, use of crystal/gemstones, Reiki, massages, healthy diet, and essential oils.

Root chakra

Common psychological symptoms of an unbalanced root chakra: loneliness, insecurities, feeling ungrounded, unconfident, abandoned, indecisive, depressed, anxious, addictions, phobias, obsessions.

Common physical symptoms of an unbalanced root chakra: lower-back pain, sciatica, varicose veins, constipation, diarrhea, rectal/anal problems, impotence, water retention, and problems with groin, hips, legs, knees, calves, ankles, and feet.

Sacral chakra

Common psychological symptoms of an unbalanced sacral chakra: eating disorders, addictions, low self-confidence, dependency issues, low libido, and unstable emotions.

Common physical symptoms of an unbalanced sacral chakra: kidney problems and urinary tract infections, chronic lower back pain, sexual disorders, infertility, gynecological problems, dysfunctional menstrual cycles, and problems with the intestines, spleen, and gallbladder.

Solar Plexus

Common psychological symptoms of an unbalanced solar plexus chakra: lack of memory and concentration, frequent fearing, feeling uncentered, sugar addictions, insomnia, and eating disorders.

Common physical symptoms of an unbalanced solar plexus chakra: digestive and intestinal disorders, indigestion, food allergies, eating disorders, poor metabolism, diabetes, obesity, eczema, acne, and other stress-related skin conditions.

Heart chakra

Common psychological symptoms of an unbalanced heart chakra: apathetic, faithlessness, unforgiving, hopelessness, distrustful, uncommitted, and detached.

Common physical symptoms of an unbalanced heart chakra: pneumonia, asthma, breast problems, respiratory problems, upper back pain, shoulder and upper arm pain, and premature aging.

Throat chakra

Common psychological symptoms of an unbalanced throat chakra: nervousness, anxiety, fear, attention deficit disorders, poor coping skills, feeling isolated.

Common physical symptoms of an unbalanced throat chakra: problems with the nasal area, irritated sinuses, sore throat, jaw pain and TMJ, voice loss, thyroid problems, teeth and gum problems, and ailments of the esophagus and tonsils.

Third-eye chakra

Common psychological symptoms of an unbalanced third-eye chakra: headaches and migraines, nightmares, seizures, neurological disorders, personality disorders and neuroses, learning difficulties, and hallucinations.

Common physical symptoms of an unbalanced third-eye chakra: eye problems, glaucoma, ear problems and hearing difficulties, spinal conditions, and scalp or hair issues.

Crown Chakra

Common psychological symptoms of an unbalanced crown chakra: depression, confusion, loss of faith, mentally disconnected, dementia, epilepsy, schizophrenia.

Common physical symptoms of an unbalanced crown chakra: light sensitivity, headaches, dementia, autoimmune disorders, neurological disorders (the crown chakra affects the health of our brains and therefore our entire mental, physical, and spiritual health).

Some yoga poses, or asanas, encourage chakra balance. (Check with your doctor before beginning a new exercise routine.) Yoga-chakras resource and videos are available through the <u>Yoga Journal</u> (See Appendix). Or, check out classes and resources at your local community center or library.

Cultivating a healthy body and mind is what maintains the asset's ability to bring the greatness that you're ready to share with the world. The asset is you. Take care of yourself. You will carry your body with you for the rest of your life. Staying in good health during transition periods is of the essence. Not only does it promote increased productivity, but it increases mental capacity for your priorities, content, and knowledge, as it fosters creativity. Understanding your dominant dosha(s), energy profile, and chakras and how they work together will help you achieve the level of wellness and health optimal for your natural mind and body composition. Thank you for taking the time today to prioritize your health, and for the improved health and success you will experience in the future.

Chapter 13:
Step 9 – Physical Environment: Make Space for Job Joy

"Your sacred space is where you can find yourself over and over again."
– Joseph Campbell

In this chapter, you will learn how to organize your physical space to maximize your creativity and productivity as they advance in your career.

Home Is Where the Heart Is

We've learned in previous chapters the importance of looking at yourself first as the starting point of any change, perspective, and progression. We've also explored your connections with the Higher Power, inner self, and your relationships with others, and how they connects to support your health and energy. What next? The ground and everything that surrounds us. Because we're living energy filled with dynamic movement, physical space influences us, and it's a reflection of our fluidity. It's a cycle that connects us from the outside in-ward. Your home tells a lot about yourself. Your home is deeply rooted in your sense of feeling secure and stable.

Home is an extension of yourself. As the saying goes: Home is where the heart is.

If you recall from our priorities, we must make space for opportunities, both in the sense of time and physical space. When I was in the early stages of my experience with reiki and understanding chakras, I learned about colors and flow of energy. Have you ever walked into a room and started feeling like you can sit and take a nap? A feeling of serenity. If you ever go to a spa, this is what you want to feel. But the opposite is also accurate. You walk into gloomy space, and you want to get out of there. Well, space plays a significant role not only in how your project yourself, but also your mind and energy.

Most of us experience the physical impact of space in terms of tidiness, cleanliness, size, and object placement. We all have different tastes in décor (modern, traditional, eclectic, etc.), but the influence goes beyond these factors. The flow of energy at home or office, help improve our health and wellbeing, balance the various aspects of our lives and help promote vitality and focus in the areas that we've identified as being high-priority, or invigorate those lacking positive energy or neglected.

Before my husband and I were engaged, we decided to move in together. As part of a new couple, you're excited that you're going to spend your time together with this beautiful person that you love. Until it hits you that, yes, it requires the actual act of merging our two worlds. Did I mention how much I dislike moving? It's beyond annoying. You know what makes it more annoying? I had been in my previous apartment for over four years after downsizing from a condo, and he had recently purchased new furniture for his apartment, which he'd been living in for a year. I must say, I thought I'd gotten rid of more stuff. I think my husband did a much better job at detaching himself from valuables very quickly. And what's worse than packing and moving? You guessed it! Unpacking. Merging and finding a new home for each of our objects required many bottles of wine to keep my sanity. (Two years ago, I was still on the "just in case I need it" method.) It was an unpleasant experience.

Then, about a year ago, we started donating or giving away the things that no longer served us or did not align with our lifestyle. You may not realize it, but having unwanted, unknown, or unserviceable items, whether you see them daily or not, has a considerable influence over your mind, clarity, and emotional states. It feels like a big fog, forgetful, and almost nonproductive. You may ask yourself, "What's making this difference?" Opening your closets may give you the answer. As I write, I realize that it's been three months since my last purging exercise. Since we recently got married, with all the gifts and purchases, it's time for it again. Hooray! I mean it. I'll share three resources that, over the last ten years, and even more, recently, shaped my attitude toward space. I was always about maintaining my space clean, but the organizing part proved to be more challenging for me.

I remember when one of my first coaching clients approached, asking me to help her put together a business plan. To respect her privacy, we will call her Marie. Marie was 39 years old, with two kids and a husband. She had a ton of ideas and was quite great at working at each and every one of her areas. From selling beauty products, to growing her cooking recipes, to event planning, she had many businesses. One of my first questions was,

"Well, which business to you want to focus or expand?" Afterall, I was hired to help her expand her business. Her answer was, *"I was hoping you'd help me on all of them. I like the things I do, but I don't have much time to focus on them."* I asked the question again, hoping to obtain a slightly different answer.

At the core of her business spread was the structure of her physical space, and lack of a vision that connected each one. Doing the things we love in life, is one of life's greatest purpose. Running a successful business while doing the things we love, however, requires focus. No surprise, she wasn't profitable enough on any of her products, to meet her financial or work/life balance goals. She found herself in back-to-back meetings, often missing key discussions and deadlines because of her lack of thinking space. She was barely home to organize her inventory of products and creating a space for them that separated them from personal belongings.

One day, we got on the phone and she was in tears. She was overwhelmed by the amount of work she had ahead and feeling fatigue in her bones. All she wanted to do was sleep. She had multiple calendars, as well as closets filled with belongings that she had since she was in her 20s, combined with collectibles belonging to her three-year-old child. Her mind was a complete fog, which for her was unusual, she thought. In reality, for years, Marie was living in a constant state of clutter; she was just missing the signs and didn't see the connections between home and office space, and how her mind was being wired to create businesses that were in the same unstructured state.

Once we were able to purge valuables that no longer served her, organize her space to be dynamic and creative, we were positioned to work on her business, which today is a successful food pantry serving thousands of New Yorkers in underserved communities. We combined her core values and business strengths into one product that yielded the greatest revenue of all: giving to others.

Exercise: Check out these scenarios, and write down the ones that apply to you. If you have been experiencing any of signs below, it may time to get organized.

1. You accidentally miss a scheduled meeting.
   Sure, this can happen for a legitimate and unpredictable reason (an earthquake, say, or a family emergency.) But what I'm talking about here is when you forget, for no good reason, that you have a routine appointment or special event planned. Especially if it happens more than once, this is a serious hint that your current system of organizing your schedule isn't working for you.

2. You don't know what you own.
   If you keep finding clothes that you don't remember buying, or you purchase books or gadgets that you forgot that you already owned (see No. 5), it's time to clean out your stuff and reorganize.

3. You keep misplacing necessities.
   Yes, everyone makes mistakes, and one-off, weird situations do happen. But if you're regularly losing track of your keys, glasses, or wallet, it means your organization routine is breaking down somewhere – quite possibly at your launchpad or in your handbag.

4. You get frustrated by mundane tasks.

   Most of us have busy lives, in which a bit of preparation is required to ensure daily tasks, like putting on makeup or making dinner, go smoothly. When these tasks become a source of stress, it's an indicator that something about the process has to change. Often, surprisingly, less is more when it comes to streamlining your mundane chores. For example, if getting dressed takes forever because you have "nothing to wear," you might have too much, and a minimalist wardrobe could be the answer.

5. You find that you're always shopping.

   Sometimes when you think you need more stuff, it's simply because the things you already own are so poorly organized that you don't realize they're there. Decluttering and organizing your belongings, especially those stashed in storage areas like closets, will clarify what you already have and whether you're unintentionally accumulating duplicates you won't use.

6. You can't locate everyday items.

   If you're always wasting time rummaging through your desk drawers, your bag, and the back of your closet, it's probably high time to establish a rule whereby everything you own has a dedicated "home." Once the habit of returning things to their proper place when you're done using them becomes second nature, the rummaging will stop.

7. You're easily distracted.

   Clutter isn't just unattractive – it can also be a big distraction. If you can't seem to get anything done, clear the clutter from your workspace and see what happens. Remember that even hidden clutter (such as a stack of documents waiting to be filed inside a storage box) can drain your mental energy. And keep in mind that confusion isn't just a problem when it comes to concentrating at work. It can also be a visual or mental obstacle to relaxation.

8. You're feeling drawn to organizing products.

   We all want miracle solutions to our problems, and we've been conditioned to think those solutions should come from a store. But although carefully chosen containers or shelves can work wonders in the right circumstances, they're not magic. Still, feeling a sudden need for new shelves and boxes can signal a real dissatisfaction with your current system of organization. It can also be a hint that you have too much stuff, and getting rid of it – rather than neatly organizing it – will make you feel better instantly.

9. You feel overwhelmed.

   At some point, almost everyone feels like they have too much to do. And you may quite literally have more items on your to-do list than the limited hours in the day allow. But you can't know for sure until you acknowledge, sort, and prioritize those items and learn to manage your time, instead of just reacting haphazardly to every task that comes your way. If you don't already have a daily routine, try creating one now.

10. You're ashamed of your space.

    If the thought of inviting a friend into your home makes you feel ashamed, or if looking at your messy desk makes you feel guilty, yup, you need to get organized. The mess may not be nearly as bad as you think once you get started.

If any of these feelings resonate with you, then it's time. If you feel stuck in your career, transitioning, or in need of enlightenment, it's yet another reason to take action.

Decluttering

You attract who you are, and physical space is a significant part of that. To attract the right opportunities, we have learned you need the right capacity. But before we jump into how we can improve the flow of energy and abundance in your space, I'd like to get you inspired by tidying up expert Marie Kondo. She's the cutest! She also wrote a book called *The Life-Changing Magic of Tidying Up: The Japanese Art of Decluttering and Organizing* (2014). She has a Netflix series, too. Each series episode carries her guests through a set of organizational steps, and it's truly a blessing to the owners of these home life changes.

You see, when you declutter, you're bringing up the emotional baggage that comes along with it. Kondo's decluttering method goes beyond organizing. It is rooted in a single question: *Does this item spark joy?* Identifying what sparks joy leads to a tidy home filled only with things you cherish. It's also a path to self-discovery, mindful living, and fulfillment. She starts by chatting with the homeowners about what they'd like to achieve. She kicks off the process by praying for the transformation that's about to occur at this home, giving gratitude for all of the items and the use each served. This notion of sparking joy and gratitude summarizes your entire career and life transformation!

Simply put, the KonMari Method follows six basic rules:

1. Commit: Committing to decluttering and organizing your space is half the battle. Once you commit yourself to tidying up your home, you can apply the method and spark more joy in your life.

2. Consider how tidying up might change your life: Before you begin the KonMari Method, ask yourself why you want to tidy up, and what your life will look like once you are done with the process. Dreaming up the outcome helps spark motivation and keeps you in check when putting things away in the future.

3. Get rid of items first: One of the critical aspects of the KonMari Method is to get rid of unwanted items first – that way, all you are left with is what needs to be organized. Before discarding, thank each item for serving its purpose.

4. Think category, not location: Another big part of the KonMari Method is tackling one thing at a time and organizing your efforts by category, not physical position. For example, it's not about cleaning out the master bedroom closet; it's about cleaning out all clothing items in the house. Or organizing all books under your roof, not just the cookbooks in your kitchen.

5. Follow the checklist order: The KonMari cleaning checklist is set up in a specific order, and you

should not stray from it. Start at the top and work your way down.

6. Find joy: It's not about getting rid of things you no longer want; it's about keeping things that spark joy. So, always think from a positive standpoint, and ask yourself if something brings you happiness, versus making a case for why it stresses you out.

Organizing Yourself

As I attempted even to consider scheduling time to get organized, I was overwhelmed by not only the urgent need to act, but also how to begin. Then, in my solutioning journey, I found a website called <u>Squirrels of a Feather</u> (See Appendix). Marissa, who's the tidy and minimalist guru, truly is an inspiration. She lost her mother to cancer at nine, and before she graduated from college, lost her father to alcoholism. So, Marissa became attached to everything. It was probably a form of having some control over things through the possessions she valued. But even with these life circumstances, she was able to find her path. Like we all can and will. She's now an inspirational minimalist, who shared a wealth of knowledge and tips on how to have, "Less stuff, more money, and be happy." Not sure about you, but I'm in! Marissa touches upon the KonMari Method, and I highly encourage you to review her useful tips, among a wealth of resources related to budgeting, and your relationship with space.

Exercise: Now that you have started making space for space (get it?), we can talk about the flow of energy in your home and even office space. It's good to get into the habit of regularly checking the flow energy in your space. One of the primary ways to check the energy flow in your home is to imagine energy as water. If water were to flow into your home – starting at the main door – where would it stop or stagnate? Ideally, the imagined water would flow harmoniously and smoothly to all areas of your home, gently refreshing it. For me, I imagine my dog excitedly running through our apartment and not hurting herself or our valuables. Use your imagination.

For the Love of Space: Feng Shui

The next nugget I'll share with you is the ancient art and science of Feng Shui. Feng Shui translates from Chinese as wind (feng) and water (shui). It's the art of arranging buildings, objects, space, and life as a method of harmonizing and bringing balance to your home or any space. Feng Shui can be used to encourage the force or energy to flow freely and create balance in space and life. For instance, an excessive amount of clutter stops us from having clarity of thought and can weigh us down emotionally.

Exercise: Okay, now that we are clear with the Feng Shui good energy basics, let's finally move some furniture and do some Feng Shui redecorating for career success! According to The Spruce (See Appendix), here are Three Easy Feng Shui Tips to Boost Your Career Energy:

1. If possible, arrange your desk in the Feng Shui commanding position (facing the door), and see if you can also face one of your lucky Feng Shui directions. The lucky directions are considered

quite important in Feng Shui as by facing them, you absorb the best quality of energy.

2. Find the North area of your office space (responsible for your Career energy), and decorate it with one or more of the following Feng Shui career success cures:

   • the map of the world.
   • a mirror in metal frame.
   • black and white photos of people whose career and energy you admire.
   • your images of career success.

3. Be sure to take good care of your energy and keep it high and vibrant by applying the Feng Shui for health tips. Feeling healthy and energized will undoubtedly help you attract better career opportunities, so be mindful of the quality of your energy at all times.

In Feng Shui, everything is viewed as being interconnected. So, if the energy feels stuck in your career, you have to make sure the energy is not held in your home. Clear out your clutter, clean the closets, check how your main door is working, etc. Often, an appropriately colored object placed within the Life Area (of your space) can help energize that space. By visually placing the <u>Feng Shui Octagon</u> (See Appendix) a tool for mapping the energies of a home or lot, over your lot plan or a floor plan of your home (starting with the first floor and then moving to any additional levels), you can figure out which parts of your home fall in which Life Areas, and then cure them with an appropriately colored object, as in this list:

Color	Home or Lot Area to Place Color	Life Area Helped	Specifically Improves
Gray	Right front	Helpful People	Assistance from others, travel
Black	Center front	Career	Career success, promotion, better job
Blue	Left front	Knowledge	Learning, spiritual growth
Green	Center left	Family	Family harmony, growth, unity
Purple	Back left	Wealth	Money, prosperity
Red	Back center	Fame	Fame and reputation
Pink	Back right	Marriage	Marriage/relationship with significant other
White	Center right	Children	Children's safety, growth, and improvement
Yellow	Center	Health	Physical, mental, and emotional health

Adapted from David Daniel Kennedy, Grandmaster Lin Yun (2018)

From painting the walls yellow in the Health Area of your home (for better health and physical wellbeing) to positioning a healthy green plant in the Family Area of your home or lot (to encourage unity and a stronger family bond), other "cures" include:

- Place an energetic fountain near your front door. The flowing energy of the water symbolizes cash, which helps more of the green stuff come your way. Get ready to enjoy more cash flow and connections with key people thanks to this simple cure.

- Clear the entryway to your home. Let the *energy* flow right into your home and life by ridding your home's front entry of obstacles. Such things as looming plants or vines, old newspapers, bikes, and toys in your front path may limit the amount of energy entering your home. Clear out anything behind your door for even more benefits.

- Make sure your home encourages learning. Put books where you can see them when you come in the front door to stimulate learning in both you and your children.

- Get rid of unwanted frustrations by fixing broken objects. Make sure your front door is in good working order. It shouldn't scrape the floor or squeak, and the doorknob, hinges, and locks should all be secure. This cure allows you to release your frustrations and anxieties and soothes your life path.

- Spice up your love life with plants in the bedroom. Place three or nine new plants in your bedroom to enliven the energy of the room, adding hope and cheer. (If the plants have pink flowers, this cure will be even stronger!)

- Position your bed to feel safe, loved, and celebrated. Place your bed in the Commanding Position of your bedroom. This spot is the one farthest from the door, but where you're still able to see the doorway and anyone approaching while you're lying in bed. Placing your bed in the Commanding Position allows you to be stronger, calmer, and in charge.

- Close drains to keep dollars from flowing out of your pockets. To keep your funds from being wasted, keep your bathroom doors closed, hang full-length mirrors on the outsides of your bathroom doors, and keep your drains closed when not in use (cover the sink drain, stop the tub, and keep the toilet lid closed).

- Encourage helpful people in your life by hanging a pleasant-sounding wind chime. The sound of a metal wind chime hung in the right-front area of your home, office, or bedroom activates more people to help you and get you more help from the people who are already at your side.

- Boost your career with a better desk position. Position your desk kitty-corner to and facing the office or cubicle door (even if you don't have an entry in your workspace). If you can't turn your desk to face the door, arrange a mirror on your desk or wall so you can see who's coming. This adjustment helps you encounter more opportunities, go further in your field, and lose less often.

I must remind you that the exercise of any life change starts with gratitude. Just like yourself, your relationships, health, or spirituality, everything has a time and place, and we must be appreciative of how all areas of our lives have served us in the past, how they may or may not today, and what they could become in the future. When you open the flow of energy around you, and you are open, you're also opening the window for the universe to replenish you, to resurface what may need to be addressed, placing you in a position of receiving the tools, resources, and relationships you need to move on to the next phase of your life. That might include necessary energy you need to apply your next steps, or the wisdom or clarity you need to figure out what it is you want to do, or help for you to find a new path, as in Marissa's story.

Regardless of your circumstances, the appreciation for your space, gratitude, and removing what no longer serves you amplifies your connection with your inner self as you become a step closer to embarking on a new journey. One must not be attached to likes or dislikes. Doing so slows down the opportunity and flow of abundance the universe and what your Higher Power has stored for you.

Remember: It all starts with you. The deeper the connection to yourself, the easier it will be to want and to attract the need for space. When your mind, body, and spirit understand the value of your creation and existence, you'll notice an urgent need to find the right home for objects, and you'll also want to maximize the use of your time. Use SMART goals to identify areas of your home or office that may need organization, decluttering, or rearranging. Set a plan, reflecting on your career goals, that's *reasonable* and *achievable*. I emphasize this, especially in this chapter, because the tasks may seem more overwhelming than most. Visualize the way you will feel after all is done, remembering that all things have served a purpose, and that one must practice gratitude.

Chapter 14:
Step 10 – Fun and Recreation:
Work Hard, Play Hard

"Everyone needs a hobby," he said. "And everyone needs a miracle or two, just to prove life is more than just one long trudge from the cradle to the grave."
— Stephen King

The goal of this chapter is for you to understand how doing more of what you love builds up your physical and mental capacity necessary to strengthen your motivation and performance at work. Getting yourself recharged through pure enjoyment is not just about getting enough sleep. It is about maintaining a wellbeing from all aspects, your mind, physical body, and your soul.

Hobbies and Leisure Time

When I ask most of my colleagues these days, "Do you have any hobbies?" or "What do you enjoy doing?" I get three types of answers. "Yes, of course, I play in a band on the weekends, I volunteer at a homeless shelter, and I'm a professional photographer!" Then you have the ones that say, "Well I don't have time for hobbies, between work and kids, it's tricky. That's life." I also get, "I don't know what my hobbies are." It's clear, by the tone and body language, who's most fulfilled. You guessed it, the ones with the enthusiastic, "Yes!" These also tend to be the ones that are agile, productive, focused, and have the most vibrant energy pouring into work. Is this always the case? No. As with everything in life, it's a dance. It's about balancing the areas of your life to assess the use of your talents at work and their alignment with your inner self.

Exercise: Answer the following self-reflective questions. As you answer, connect with your inner child and follow your feelings and inward energy when responding.

- What are your favorite things to do? (i.e., sports, games, vacationing and traveling and or personal expression such as art, music, dance, meditation, etc.)?
- Where and when do you participate: at home, in your community, outside of your natural environment?
- With whom do you interact, and how important is socializing in your leisure time?
- How does technology affect your leisure?
- How does your leisure impact your social networks?
- Are you actively involved in your leisure subculture?
- As a result of your leisure, are you actively involved in your community?

Next, how do you prioritize fun and recreation? You may refer to your wheel of life.

- Why is your leisure important/unimportant to you?
- How does leisure make you feel?
- What do you value about your leisure? (What is important or unimportant?)
- What role does leisure play in your life (family or friends' life, work or school life, community or subcultural life)?
- Do you closely identify with people of similar leisure interests? Meaning, is leisure as important in your life as your family and work time? What are the benefits you associate with leisure?
- What do you do for yourself (not including others) out of pure enjoyment?
- Are these things aligned with your dosha?
- What leisurely dreams you wish would come true? What would you do? Where would you want to go? Would you want anyone with you? If so, who and why? Why is it important? What is preventing you?

Research shows, time after time, that having time for recreation, hobbies, and just plain old fun is key to career success. It's the way we recharge. It's a form of grounding. It's the source of creativity and personal growth. Put energy into things that get you lost creatively, otherwise that same energy will naturally gravitate to self-destructive areas such as aggression and anger. It's like signing children up for karate, baseball, or gymnastics classes to keep their energy busy; we should follow this notion as adults, too.

When I'm tired and burnt out, I don't enjoy many parts of my life. My perspective is clouded, even my judgment. Let me share my experience: When I was writing this book, at some point, I lost motivation. Why? I was exhausted. I had not taken a break from work, I had family commitments, and I was only getting rest when I slept. I was falling asleep as I was writing! Not cool. Without the appropriate playtime, you will compromise even the things you find to be fun and bring fulfillment. Note: It's essential to take the time to identify when you feel most fulfilled.

One of my best friends is at her highest when she surrounds herself with people, certainly in a social setting. It fuels her to be outside and actively engaged. I often call her the energizer bunny. As I'm writing this, she's texting me: "Good morning sunshine (sun emoji) and happy Monday!!!!!" (yes, five exclamation points). This is her all day, every day. She introduced me to how to feel fun by getting lost in the moment about seven years ago. I had been a grandma at best.

I remember our first snowboarding trip together. She asked if I wanted to try it, she sent me an essentials list, and there we were, on a bus to a snow sport vacation. I don't even like the cold! It was one of the best experiences of my life. It was a combination of newness, adventure, and doing something that was certainly out of reach for me. Ever since, we've been unstoppable: hiking trips, biking tours, all-day self-made walking tours of the city, painting – she even tried a singing class, although she already has a fantastic voice. Our creative juices and energy grew exponentially.

I've experienced the most significant leaps in my career when my fun tank was full, and I spend my free time enjoying myself. But with all the fun and excitement also comes recharging. Your body must replenish to function to its full capacity. We all do it differently, and the source of energy comes in all different shapes, as we've learned with our doshas.

Keeping Our Energy Aligned

What I find interesting is that many of us look forward to Friday all week long! We find freedom during our free time, but then we go home and do chores, the same routine. By the time we're done, it's Sunday, and we're saddened by the thought of going back to work. A couple of things to note:

1. We don't have to wait until the weekend to do the things we love. Accomplish them during the weekdays (or whatever your work schedule accommodates). You'll feel the reward of having more short-term balance. I can feel exhausted on Mondays after coming from a weekend of all fun, because my body doesn't have enough time to adjust to the shenanigans I've crammed in over less than two days.

2. Finding pleasure in the chores and the mundane is critical. A way to do this is by practicing gratitude as you cook, clean, beg the kids to do homework. Why is this important? The odds are, there's a lot more of this than actual recreation time. Don't waste precious time waiting for the "big" enjoyments.

3. Take a look at your use of free time. We learned through Soforic's wealth lessons that your use of free time is essential to determining your path to financial freedom, but the same holds to any part

of your life. Your free time is a treasure that one uses wisely. Whether to take a vacation or have "me time", it must be well spent and in alignment with your life priorities.

The more we become one with our physical, mental, and spiritual sides, the more we will see the progression as it relates to our hobbies, careers, and life experiences. Hobbies and times of enjoyment are an essential component to our career development. It reveals itself in many ways, regardless of your circumstances. *Activities can be significant or small. It can be anything, really.* Here are a few reasons for prioritizing this area of your life as you dedicate time to a career path.

Why Have Fun?

One of my very wise sisters-from-another-mother and best friend reminded me of this recently. The beauty of life is that we can find enjoyment in pretty much anything we do. If you think about it, most of the time, your day-to-day activities (even if you love your job) wouldn't go into the category of fun and recreation. However, we can find joy in our relationships, taking care of our health through exercising or playing a sport, volunteering, reading books, taking a class, going to church; really, any area of your life can easily fall into this space. When you've thoughtfully identified them, prioritize them according to where you seek opportunity in your wheel of life.

You Will Attract Abundance

The more time you dedicate to the things and the people in life that bring joy, the more your body feels empowered to be creative, find ways to give, collaborate with others, and exude your authentic self. Whether you share through passion, innovation, productivity, or care, your energy changes and levels will show what it is precisely meant to do. The balance between survival work, that is, the work you get paid to do, versus efforts expended for self-fulfillment manifests and creates energy balanced between worlds. Thus, directly and indirectly, this has an impact on your productivity. So when you see yourself lying on your surfboard, or sitting at the park with a book, know that you're doing yourself and the world a favor.

Hobbies Are Meant to Free Enjoyment for Yourself

Families and day-to-day chores may take up a ton of our weekends and evenings. However, hobbies, specifically, are meant to bring self-joy. Yes, self, meaning "you". Take an opportunity to only be responsible for yourself for once. For me, that means painting and writing. It's all about me, my thoughts, and I. It feels mindless, just like when I'm meditating or sitting at the beach just hearing the waves. Hobbies can also serve as a battery booster. So if you have a hobby that also helps you relax mentally and physically, you have found a winner!

Opportunity to Meet Others on the Same Wavelength

When I visit Mont Lawn City Camp to volunteer, not only am I giving and receiving sparks of awesomeness from the kids, but the mentors and staff are all on the same wavelength. We can all have different personalities, talents, and tastes, but there's something about assembling a group of people with common interests. An explosion of energy and love towards a single vision creates childlike moments. Similarly, my husband and I recently went to see the US Grand Prix, and when he asked me about my favorite part, I said there was something about being there with a bunch of track fans that made the day extra special.

The Power of Knowledge

Whether you've had a hobby for a long time or just started picking something up, there's power in knowledge. Gaining a new skill set or indulging in learning a new activity not only creates new circuitry in your brain, but opens you to see new opportunities and learn about talents you never thought you had. You might also learn about some pursuits you didn't know you had any interest in. I remember my best friend bought me a painting toolkit soon after our first experience at a "paint night." I thought to myself, *I can make a mess and have a cocktail at the same time? Sure, I'll take it!* But I was able to gain so much from it. I painted over forty paintings in two years. I emerged into my paintings. I would watch the Art Sherpa (whom I highly recommend) on YouTube. She's fantastic, with such an excellent spirit, and most of my paintings came about through her teachings. She taught me to write prayers and messages on my canvases before I start painting. Now each time I look at any of my paintings, each reminds me of a greater good, a broader mission, and the wishes I have for the world and myself. In case you're wondering, the cover of this book is indeed one of my paintings. It hangs in our dining room every day and night. My wish to the world on this piece of art, expresses the desire for each and everyone of us to bring who we truly are to this world. That each person that takes a look at the painting immediately connects with their authentic self with love and compassion.

As Bob Ross, a painting guru, once stated, "I started painting as a hobby when I was little. I didn't know I had any talent. I believe talent is just a pursued interest. Anybody can do what I do." One could say, "That's a joke!" Have you seen the man? I used to watch him for hours as a child, and now his TV reruns have gone viral. But Bob is spot on. The pursuit of an interest becomes an essential part of achieving life's abundance; there's no right or wrong in the action itself.

Becoming More Well-Rounded

Trying new things, having a hobby, and finding joy in areas outside of work or even home opens you up to what else exists out there, beyond your comfort or familiarity zones. It better connects you to your inner self, but also to the endless opportunities that exist when you're not confined by the usual limits. When I first started painting, it forced me to seek and better understand others' visual experiences in order to appropriately connect with others using cues that inspired gratitude and love on a wider audience. You become more in touch with the fact that your world is not the only world, and there are multiple worlds for a reason. As a result, you become better at understanding where people are coming from, not in a physical sense, but in terms of their experience, values, spirit, and life journey, helping you to create a medium of respect and admiration for others. Also, this growth allows for flexibility toward life's sometimes inexplicable nuances.

A Shift in Perspective

When you find a sacred space that understands you, that allows you to get lost and also to come back to reality, you have a greater appreciation for life and the beauty and abilities it brings your way. It helps you balance between more pressing matters and the cloud you feel when you're in the presence of joy. Coming out of any routine and into a space that allows you to exercise a different part of your brain provides a clearer perspective on what's essential in life. It also promotes a calmer place when stressful situations arise, because you can appreciate and know that there's more out there, beyond just the problems.

Your Whole Mind

As I continue finding new perspectives, I found an enjoyable read that I'd recommend: Daniel Pink's *The Whole New Mind: Why Right-Brainers Will Rule the Future* (2006). Wow! For someone like myself, whose natural tendencies tend to gravitate toward logic, analysis, and being more methodical, this book encourages the use of more creative means to drive concepts and promote creativity. When I read it, I had recently picked up some hobbies, like painting and playing guitar (which reminds me – I never finished guitar classes). I started feeling the power of fun, playfulness, and how it influences your career and your productivity at work.

In his book, Pink describes six specific high-concept and high-touch aptitudes that have become essential in this new era. Being able to balance between playtime and work enhances these high concept/touch aptitudes; many are considered soft or non-core competencies. The six senses are: Design, Story, Symphony, Empathy, Play, and Meaning.

- The need for function, but also for *design*. Today it is economically crucial and personally rewarding to create something that is also beautiful or emotionally engaging.
- The need for not just argument, but also *story*. Data isn't enough. The essence of persuasion, communication, and self-understanding has become the ability to narrate a compelling story.
- The need for not just focus, but also *symphony*. While the industrial society specialized in making a few things in large numbers, the conceptual age is about putting the pieces together – symphony. Not analysis but synthesis – seeing the big picture, crossing boundaries, and being able to combine pieces into an arresting new whole.
- The need for not just logic, but also *empathy*. In addition to logic, you need to have an ability to understand what makes your fellow man tick, to forge relationships, and to care for others.
- Not just seriousness, but also *play*. There is evidence of enormous health and professional benefits of laughter, lightheartedness, games, and humor.
- The need for not just accumulation, but also *meaning*. Materialism has freed people from day-to-day struggles to pursue more significant desires: purpose, transcendent, and spiritual fulfillment – the high-concept, high-touch abilities that matter most are fundamentally human attributes.

There's an underlying theme with all of Pink's transitions. Each sense moves us to a more connected desire, one that connects to a person's inner child and sense of play.

Life as a Playground

Ever since I can remember, the workforce has promoted more work. Forget play. I remember having jobs where employees were encouraged to stay late for optics and promotion opportunities. Optics? Colleagues stayed late to finish their errands online, while also getting reimbursed for dinner for staying late. Was this the case for many of us? No. It promoted already overdriven, unbalanced behavior to be rewarded by focusing on work, plus overextending yourself, which later led to burnout. It shifted the opportunity to seek change to a mindset of efficiency. It also encouraged the notion that one has to choose between career success or personal life when, in actuality, you can effectively achieve both.

I learned that optics became a personal barrier affair. We may encounter the wise souls who tell you, "Don't work too hard." But for me, that translates to, "I need to work smarter while still achieving business and personal objectives." In turn, this places a hard stop when I can engage in work versus playtime or me time, in general. You'll learn this in Soforic's *Wealthy Gardener* (2019), which has an impressive, more aggressive view on this topic. I'm impartial. Soforic's dream was financial freedom, and therefore, his life plan allocated more time to effort early on in his life. Prioritizing by phase is much more attainable and achievable than thinking of your priorities downward each day. As I shared, I have entered a period of marriage or nesting and personal growth through writing this book, and engaging in activities promote creativity. So, playtime here I come! It's been a while, and I miss you.

The Atlantic (Khazan, 2019) recently released an article that stated:

"This culture of overwork has well-known personal consequences. Working more than fifty-five hours a week raises the risk of heart attack and stroke. People who work longer hours tend to be more anxious and depressed, and their sleep suffers. Long hours aren't even good for performance: As Schulte indicated in the *Harvard Business Review,* research has shown that people's IQ drops thirteen points when they're in a state of tunnel-vision busyness."

So, overworking without sufficient playtime makes you intellectually less competent, too. I can attest that simple tasks or even feelings don't surface as they should when we're not looking inward. For instance, I have experienced the inability to feel pleasure or see the softer attributes of life. Those are the moments when I'm disconnected, too focused on the to-do lists, the external world. You see, only when you connect to your inner self, with your Higher Power, are you genuinely able to feel pleasure for what it is. It happens when you meet true love, and always starts and ends with gratitude. When you're ready to appreciate any day of the week that you're off or free, when you're able to seek enjoyment in any activity you may be performing, and understand the nuances of the world that has been given to you, then the world becomes a big playing field. We start shifting our perspective to one of enjoyment and fun, pleasure, and everything else becomes one.

But it's also beyond just work itself. Our generation is always connected through all sorts of devices, and because we do it with ease, with the Alexa's of the world reminding us of our beloved to do's, we often book our entire days, simply because we can! There are some weeks, especially during the summer, where I spend very little to no time just sitting quietly, with nothing on my calendar. Remember: Without the appropriate time to connect with yourself, you will lose sight of what's essential for your purpose. Time will feel like it flies, because you're not allowing it to flow at its intended pace.

If you understand that your time is limited on this earth, then perform this **exercise:**

1. Look at your calendar for the next three weeks (if it's not happening then, it probably won't be happening later).
2. What percentage of your time is dedicated to each of the areas of your wheel of life?
3. What proportion is allocated to fun, recreation, leisure?
4. What percentage of hobbies are active, that connect or fulfill one of the wheels of life components, versus inactive, such as watching TV, Pinterest browsing (guilty!).

Still, it is important to note that play doesn't only refer to leisure or time you consciously choose to designate as fun. Instead, using life as a playground and applying the same feelings and intent to day-to-day activities. Then life is not split into working or projects; life becomes whole.

Ideally, we want to engage most of our leisure time in areas that also actively encourage development and joy in other areas of life, especially those that you have prioritized when assessing your wheel of life. Inactive or passive time is occasionally needed; who doesn't mind a Netflix binge evening after a tough day at work? But excessive use does develop distance between your inner self and your connection with the external world.

In this chapter, we've learned and acknowledged the benefits of prioritizing fun, recreation, and leisure, within our life plan. Using leisure time to connect with other life aspects reaps the most significant benefits and fulfillment. Remember: Gratitude plays a crucial role in our ability to feel joy, since active leisure activities also require work or commitment, like trying your best to make it to Pilates when you really just want to go home and eat dinner (Monika [my instructor], thank you for inspiring us to want to go to class!). Develop SMART goals to adjust according to your life priorities and interests. Now, step away and enjoy one of your favorites!

Chapter 15:
Your Fear Is a Spirit, and How to Overcome It

"Our deepest fear is not that we are inadequate. Our deepest fear is that we are powerful beyond measure. It is our light not our darkness that most frightens us."
— Marianne Williamson

Wow! You have learned so much, and you have made strides! But you may feel fear, insecurities, time issues, and obligations creeping in. Fear is a spirit, and it's the opposite if love. Only these two energies exist, and then every emotion, feeling, thought, and action becomes a manifestation and perspective of these two spirits. As Teilhard de Chardin said, we're spirits living a physical experience. This chapter will remind you of the common barriers that we both know will come up throughout your journey, in an attempt to prevent you from achieving your career goals.

We're are human, after all. Resistance originating from lack of accountability or planning fears (we're too old or busy, have insufficient skills, need to make financial adjustments, etc.) – you'll experience it all. Your ego's job is to protect you, and it will make sure to keep you in the safest environment, which is where you are today. No change. Yes, ego promotes standardized behavior, whether it is positive or negative. It works from prior experience or knowledge, which is why we so often resist change. So much so that we fear even success.

Let's take a look at the fears and very creative excuses that will surface during each component of the SmartRise system. At some level, you may still feel some of these thoughts, or even lingering doubts throughout this entire process. Perform a sanity check on all areas of your wheel of life to determine what's triggering the fear or doubt to the surface, acknowledge this, and then choose to toss or address it. Remember: There's always a next step, so the goal is to keep moving forward with the content or information you have, and to press forward. There's a popular phrase in Spanish, "No mires hacia atrás ni para coger impulso." In English, that translates to: Don't look back, not even to gain momentum. Don't look back, not even to gain momentum.

Acknowledging Your Fears and Letting Go

Fears are a natural emotion that can surface at any moment, so be ready. It will happen. It is a mechanism of our ego to protect us. It does its job very well, and it is there with good intent. The key is to acknowledge that it is there (and if it's there, to ask yourself why it is there), and then to let it go (master it by addressing the cause or otherwise having it take a back seat). You can connect with your inner self, your Higher Power, and have a dialogue. Someone who lets fear in the door is giving it power to decide on their behalf.

You have a plan, so own it. You have talents and yourself as the asset, so value yourself. You have the world and back of things, people, and circumstances to be thankful for. Be grateful. You have tools to empower yourself, take care of your health, give and receive, embrace your relationships, and reach financial freedom. Use them. Remind yourself of the consequences of not moving forward. Once you have a taste of what movement and advancement feel like, you will have no regrets for any of the work and determination you've invested so far. Practice exercises presented earlier in the book to open up your crown and sacral chakras. It will help clear up any negative thoughts, open you up to a true connection with your Higher Power, and increase your confidence to achieve the goals you have set forth for yourself.

You Don't Know What You're Passionate About

If you feel like you still don't have a good sense of what you're passionate about, think again. You have lived some of a life span. There are reasons why you wake up in the morning other than your problems and issues. Continue practicing gratitude, specifically focusing on being grateful for the way your Higher Power designed you. You were designed for a purpose, and to help achieve a mission. Circumstances, people, and thoughts will come your way that will ignite the areas of your life that bring you joy.

Spend time understanding your dosha(s). Make sure your lifestyle, exercise, health, and activities are in alignment with your mind-body type. Practice exercises that open up your solar plexus, which is the source of creativity, creation, and pleasure. This is a time to focus your attention on hobbies and fun activities that bring you joy. Ultimately, it will help to increase focus on yourself, and in being able to add words and actions to your definition of passion.

You're Too Busy to Focus on a Career Change

You may think the system or career change, in general, is not for you. Let me break something to you. You choose how to spend your time. You can choose to live a life that's specifically framed for you, or choose to live a life like others, or just as you are now. Career change goes in the same bucket as having babies: there's never a perfect time. You do it or not. You may think there are ideal circumstances, but without uprooting yourself, you'll remain stuck.

Take a look at your wheel of life. Assess the areas that you'll be focusing on during this season of your life. Rethink what areas of your life are pulling the others out of whack. The greatest gift of all to you as a creation of love is to use your talents and share. Practice mindfulness through grounding exercises like meditation or yoga. Maybe seeking further knowledge like Akashic Records or Reiki will surface any blockages that need to be addressed for you to declutter your mind, body, and space. It will allow for greater focus on all areas of your life, and for spending time doing what's designed for you, as well as the things you love.

You Don't Want to Close Doors

A job goes beyond the functions, the work, the deliverables, the meetings. It's more so in relationships. Relationships not only keep most of us employed, but if you're like me, my greatest love and friendships originated from work. Maintaining a respectful, transparent relationship with your current or prior working life is always an opportunity as long as the intent and action are win-win. Acknowledging your work and personal growth priorities, regardless of whether you are seeking a new opportunity or not, is key at all times. Work will revolve around performance, areas of focus, and overall engagement in the workforce or with clients. Take a look at your strengths using your Fascination Advantage Profile. Make sure you create a brand for yourself. The doors will always remain open when employers or clients see value.

Remember: The extent of the relationships can and will evolve like any other. Practice exercises that open up your heart and throat chakras, for effective communication, integrity, and discipline as you continue preparing the next steps of your career. A career transition is an important time-critical to maintain your health at optimal levels. Including practicing self-care and ensuring you're at your peak performance when you depart.

You Worry That You Won't Make Enough Money

We learned that income could come from many sources. Also, your strengths and values can be branded based on your fascinate and energy profiles. Craft key selling points that can be used during resumes, interviews, or when negotiating with employers. Give and contribute. It sounds counterintuitive, but you will ignite the cycle for receiving. Consider all the possible ways that you can give and start giving. Gratitude, gratitude, gratitude. Be grateful for both today's and tomorrow's assets.

If you are transitioning to a lower-paying field or becoming independent, trust that you will be successful in the new space. Your career and or budget plans should reflect your ongoing targets. Two things can happen. Either your costs must go down to accommodate the shift in income; or, you must identify a second source of income until you complete your transition. Refer to passive income content to identify areas that may surprise you. You can turn hobbies into income! Know that, over time, you will reach your target. Practice exercises that open up your root chakra. It will help facilitate a feeling of growing and security throughout this process.

You Don't Think That There Are Any Jobs out There

There is a job out there. Remember: Look inward first, with you as the key asset, the package of talents and skills, and then look outward. Instead of focusing on the job or job description that inspires you, consider reviewing companies where you would like to work first. I have met and coached many individuals that have created their job once they have a foot in the door. Eventually, I attracted what was best for me over time. If it doesn't exist, create it.

This is the time to review your career plan and road-maps and assess that you have the appropriate pathway to where you want to be at each interval. You may feel that you're not there yet, but you will be if you stick to the process. Don't take your hobbies for granted. Review the gap analysis portion of your plan, to identify and review the necessary steps to get you to the place you want to reach. Practice inner child and Higher Power dialogue to understand and obtain confirmation that will inform your next steps. Practice exercises that open up your Third-Eye chakras to clear your vision, intuition, and attacking. It will help you see opportunities with clarity, like lifting a veil that has been covering your eyes for so long.

You Don't Think You Can Do It, Because You're on Your Own

You have more than you think. You have relationships, so leverage all of them: Higher Power, inner child, yourself; close relationships, specifically those that lift you, whether those are friendships, coworkers, your partners, or your dog. Thanks to my dog, I've been able to write this book; she's been at my feet the whole time, keeping me warm, but also reminding me that there's a world out there, ready to read this thing, so I need to keep pushing forward! Some of you may want to explore mentors and coaches. Or you can choose someone that not only will inspire you, but can also guide and tweak your plan along the way so that you're solely focused on the doing part. That's cool, too.

It's like going to the gym. You can choose to learn how to use the equipment or learn the workouts to do on your own – great. Identify your needs and integrate it into your plan. Needing others is not a sign of weakness, it is one of surrendering your ego, and letting yourself take up all the resources you need to continue your awesomeness journey. Take the opportunity to network. Perhaps outside of your comfort zone, engage with those on the same wavelengths through hobbies or your community engagement. Practice exercises that promote energy flow, like Reiki. Practice exercises that open up your sacral and throat chakras for the flow of information, content, and personal empowerment. You got this!

You Have Done the Same Job for a Long Time Now, and Don't Think You Are Qualified for Anything Else

You have identified your strengths, talents, and, more importantly, the fact that you do not want to continue doing the same thing. Regardless of what stage you are at within your career, or in terms of seniority at your organization, knowledge is gold. There's always the opportunity to seek new skills and knowledge. Especially when you're in the cusp of a transition, be creative and put your skills to perhaps a different use than you have in the past. Industries and organizations often have crosscutting functions that are much more dependent on organizational competencies than traditional technical or credential-dependent functions.

For example, I transitioned from working for a Wall Street business in the area of operations management. I happened to gravitate and was assigned to work in the healthcare sector. Months later, I learned my heart was in helping create systems, and eventually moved full-time to healthcare. Think about transferable competencies before you see qualifications as a limitation. Practice exercises that open up your sacral and solar plexus chakras for self-empowerment and creativity.

You Think You Are too Old to Make a Change

Be grateful for the age, your path, your journey, and the fact that you are the age you are, with the wealth of knowledge and support you have. Start with yourself. There's no such thing as being too old to choose a path forward to fulfillment. You have an unknown number of years remaining to live, to truly live in your purpose, not wasting your time working to please others, or performing activities that no longer serve you. You have a plan that outlined a phased and gradual roadmap. It's more important than ever to practice gratitude so that you start feeling the changes that are occurring around you. Practice exercise to open up your root and third-eye chakras. It will facilitate the flow of grounding, knowing that timing is always right. Also, it opens up the ability to see things for what they truly are. Regardless of your age, health and space maintenance is of the essence; it attracts the things that are appropriate for you, and also is always setting you up for the next phase of your career and life journey.

You Worry that Changing Your Career Will Harm Your Marriage

As presented early in this book, being on board with your partner is key. You both commit to becoming a unified front, and changes in your career shouldn't be excluded from your life plan. You each have individual paths, but one that you share and bring to each other each day. Work-life balance is the most common area that tends to be compromised during a career transition, followed by a lack of communication. Remember: A solid relationship is a partnership when you talk about planning for life aspects, like career or finances, and there's an underlying, fundamental layer that must be in place at all times. This layer is composed of each individual's core values and your love. Referring to each of your core values, speaking each other's love language sets the tone for everything else in marriage.

A career change is the key area worth discussing. Understanding each other's journeys before you were together, but also the future that you envision, is just as essential. Your plan should reflect a collaborative integration of your marriage's goals and objectives. Include what's important for you together, but also as individuals. Discussing, deciding, and planning together ensures early engagement throughout the entire process. During this time, it's important to fill each other's love tanks, because it's a period of transition and a major life event. Revisit your relationships and your fun or recreation goals together. Practice exercise (if together, even better) that opens up the throat, heart, and solar plexus chakras. It will encourage open and transparent communication, love and appreciation for what each partner brings to the marriage, as well as creativity and pleasure, as you enjoy this process as you look forward to the outcomes.

Kicking Fear to The Side When You Have a System

What do you have to lose? Regardless of the fear that will surface for you, ask yourself the question, "What do you have to lose?" Is it your sanity, relationships, personal fulfillment, or health? Maybe you're losing your most important asset: yourself. So many of us live without living, assuming "this is it". There's more to life, and you know it. Be grateful for being a person who does not lose herself. Set the path forward for others who have the same circumstances as you, the same doubts and fears, and serve as the example that, just as it was possible for you, it will be possible to them.

So, what can go wrong with the SmartRise System? Let's take a look.

Step 1: Career Planning: It may feel overwhelming, and you start getting a sense that this is becoming real. It is. When you think the hesitating and fear are creeping up, pause and identify the source of the hesitation. Is it the format? Is it a part of the content? Don't give up. Remember: You are worth every effort, and the more you do now, the less work it will be later. Opportunities will line up with the full lifestyle strategy you have learned; you will become a magnet for the right opportunities, and your perspective will come from a place of abundance.

However, if you find that you don't regularly use a plan, considering breaking it up into weekly or monthly achievement or goals as you build up to the broader framework. People who do not complete the career plan usually do not follow through in a disciplined way. Review your priorities again, and assess your losses and gains from completing this process. Don't get stuck with the format. The *content* is the driver of the steps that you need to reach your goals.

Step 2: Making it Happen: You may start to have feelings of anxiety and question your ability to continue moving forward. Most people get stuck at this phase because they are not following the fundamental components of the process, like understanding core values, talents, and seeing themselves as the asset. More importantly, they are stuck in their old ways of prioritizing. We learned from Steven Covey that the phrases "I have" or "I need" come from a place of being reactive. We want to be proactive and understand it's okay to say no, or spend less time doing things of lesser priority. People stuck at this step often think they need something else to accomplish it. Just keep pressing forward. Connect with your Higher Power and inner guides to lessen the burden of the process, and to help you follow the steps that work best for you. Leverage your energy profile and Fascination Profile types to gain a greater appreciation for the kind of person you are. Continue practicing gratitude and gaining insights into your likes and dislikes.

Step 3: Personal Growth and Self-Management: You may experience extreme fatigue, fogginess, and feelings that you may have never felt before; this one of the most common barriers when people reach this step. Afterall, we rarely are taught to learn about ourselves. This may be the first time you are even thinking or asking yourself some of these very complex questions.

I often imagine going through a magnetic field, trying to cross over to the other side, while every ounce of energy is being sucked out of your soul. If it sounds ridiculously consuming, know that it gets better, and then the opposite will happen. You will be bursting with energy, knowing you are acting at your highest level. You will learn more about yourself and will be okay with others questioning that you are different or have some new hobbies or talents, or that maybe you see the world differently.

Don't be surprised if you raise eyebrows throughout this step and ongoing. Life is meant to be a constant change, and you are designed to be the best version of yourself all day, every day. The more you embrace versus resist the change, the easier this process will be. Resting and being kind to yourself is very important during this step.

Step 4: Financial prosperity: This is probably the funniest step of all. Why is it funny? First, because it's either the one that people think they are really good at, or they have a different impression of their relationship with money. People that often are stuck at this step may not have full visibility of where the money is going. So being open to the outcome, and to discovering that money may be going to things and material goods that are not aligning with your life priorities, is suggested. Second, people may focus too much on the actual dollar, the figure in their bank account. This process is focused on understanding your assets, expenses, and aligning with your career goals. Practicing patience with yourself and the process is critical.

Building financial freedom takes time and discipline; any attempt to short cut the process by skipping steps or committing to a get-rich-quick scheme will only create a delay. Focusing on life changes that will only get you closer to your financial goals is recommended.

Step 5: Inner Connection: It may create anxiety and doubts to surrender or even to trust that something beyond you can have such an influence over your life. During this step, readers may experience doubts and start questioning the mere existence of any power that they can find within. Living life thinking external resources are the *only* resources creates limitations for yourself and others. Remember: The most significant insight and wisdom comes from The Unknown. And the human mind can only create based on our past experiences and the thoughts of others. Do you really think that the most fabulous and most talented people in our generation did it only because their brains generated this magical idea? No. Tapping into your inner resources allows finesse, ease, and exponential growth for any process.

Step 6: Relationships: This step may be either very easy, for some, or create anxiety for others. Me included. I am certainly more of an introvert, although I have traits of extroversion as well. I particularly enjoy alone time, and because my energy is all about achieving, and checking off boxes, I tend to bypass or not use relationships that would have helped me get there even faster. Furthermore, your support network is at the center of any career. It's there to support you; accepting our gifts and friendships, and having a collaborative relationship with our peers, makes things easier in all sorts of ways. It is vital to invest time and to have a sincere interest in others. Practicing empathy and compassion will lift others as well as yourself.

Step 7: Contribution and Community: A common misconception is thinking that you may be too busy or not have much to give. Having your mindset come from a place of abundance helps you to realize that you can give in a bunch of ways. You can start by using your primary love language to give. You may also question that "give, and you shall receive" part, initially. When you start giving, you inherently begin the cycle of abundance and receiving into your life. You will feel a sense of not only self-fulfillment but an immediate understanding of it. This is "my thing" after all. You start seeing your talents and gifts in ways that you may have never experienced before, but also feel the reward. Practicing gratitude and observing how your perspective may be shifting are ways to stay focused and seek every opportunity to give and contribute.

Step 8: Health and Wellness: A common barrier in this step is that many of us only prioritize our health when we lack it. Working from a place of being preventive is critical here. Because you're the most crucial asset, compromising your health is the equivalent of being a photographer with a broken camera. Even worse, you cannot replace yourself. You can delegate and believe that there are ways, but the reality is there's only one person like you in the world. Intentionally. We need you.

People also immediately and thoughtlessly jump to diet and exercise; this is not the key component of staying healthy. Instead, work from a place that aligns with your doshas and energy profile, in an environment that meets your mind and body where you are. Second, but as important, is that the more you practice self-care, the more you can read or listen to your body. You will learn to focus on the right activities at the right place. Because we're pure energy, we must be patient with how our minds and bodies react to the gradual changes. During a career transition or any transition, we're in a vulnerable state, and it is not surprising that we experience colds, aches, and mental or emotional responses. More than ever, nurture and love your health.

Step 9: Physical Environment: The most common sticking point during this step is that it is considered tedious, and so readers often don't prioritize working through the process. Similar to the Contribution and Community step, it is often hard to initiate the process, but you will quickly reap the benefits. It's undoubtedly a giving, but also a high-reward part of the process. Energy flows inward, within, and outward. Our composition feeds from space and flow. Without space and flow, our lives will encounter roadblocks, and your transition may seem slow and cumbersome. It's essential to have a plan, use resources, and tricks (such as the KonMari Method) to work through the space and make it friendly. You can start with tips that influence your career, but be sure that you complete the process in a bundle, that is, in a weekend or a few hours at a time. It will help highlight and shed light and energy full steam, and support your aspirations in the future.

Step 10: Fun and Recreation: Yay for fun! Believe it or not, as joyful as fun time is, you will typically experience neglect in this area during a career transition. You may think to yourself, *I can't take time off, or splurge financially*, or you may still feel unstable. We learned that fun, recreation, and hobbies can be found in both little and big things. Waiting for that vacation or that yearly retreat may be significant and something to look forward to, but you can make the most of the time until then, too.

Finding joy in day-to-day activities allows you to flow freely and to respond best to life's downers that inevitably come our way. Focusing the time for yourself or enjoyment with others demonstrates your ability to value yourself. It can also be a reward for sticking to your plan. It's recommended that you practice identifying one way to find enjoyment at least once a day, while planning for that trip to Italy that you have been looking forward to, as a reward for working and committing to prioritizing what's important to you. You will be happier, and, as we learned, "smarter" coming out of it.

We all have instances of regret, fear, and anxiety. But unlike many others, you now have the tools and practices to punch fear to the sidelines effectively. You have a bigger mission to accomplish, rather than dwelling on the limitations and perceptions of others. You have an individual path to follow, and so not allowing your authentic self to come out, play, work, and be itself will be your biggest regret. Not following through with this system is like deliberately stopping yourself from fulfillment, from not meeting the only purpose we have in life: to be ourselves and live it.

By this time, you should have sufficient SMART goals for each of your life areas to formulate a self-care plan. Refer to the checklist below, outlining examples of outcomes you should be looking to achieve. Since you're the most meaningful asset of all, we need to make sure you care for it, beyond all priorities.

Stay on Track!: Self-Care Checklist

Exercise: Check off the outcomes in this list that you are doing or planning to achieve and note the ones that you aren't doing what you'd like to add to your plan.

Relationships

- I am actively working on improving all of my relationships.
- I am aware of my own negative relationship patterns and am actively working on healing and changing these so I can be closer to others.
- I have let go of the relationships (if any) that drag me down.

- I am focused on how I can be more loving and kinder with the people in my life.
- I share appreciation with those I love, my friends and family, throughout the day.
- I do not gossip or talk negatively about others. If I talk about others, it is to share what I love about them.
- I am honest and direct with people in my life.
- I am open to resolving conflict in a healthy and loving way.
- I do not judge or criticize others.
- I do not "take personally" the things that people say to me or their reactions.
- I am dependable; I do what I say I'm going to do.
- I have a best friend, someone whom I can share anything with.
- I am able to speak my truth and set loving boundaries with others (a boundary is what *you* will do to take care of yourself in the face of someone else's behavior).

Inner Connection and Spirituality

- I know that I am a spiritual being living in a human body.
- I feel a deep connection with my spiritual connection.
- I feel a sense of support and unconditional love from my spiritual connection. I know that I am not alone.
- I have activities I do on a regular basis that nurture my spiritual life.
- I have faith that my life is unfolding exactly as it should for my highest good.

Wellness, Physical and Emotional Health

- I get adequate sleep every night.
- I eat healthy meals regularly.
- I carry health bars with me for a boost if I am hungry during the day.
- I drink lots of water throughout the day.
- I walk or exercise at least three times per week.
- I rarely eat sugar.
- I rarely drink alcohol.
- I rarely use caffeine.
- I am actively taking care of any physical conditions I have.
- I get a massage on a regular basis.
- I feel peaceful and happy with my life.
- I have resolved past issues and live fully in the present.
- I know my own intrinsic worth and lovability – I know I am **fabulous**!
- I am free of any resentment and am not holding any other person responsible for my happiness and well-being.
- I am able to easily forgive others and see their behavior with compassion.
- I am pursuing my dreams and living my purpose.
- I feel my life has balance, and that I have plenty of time to do all that I want to.

Physical Environment

- My home is well organized and clean.
- I live in a home that I love.
- The way my house is decorated uplifts my spirit.

- My home is clutter free.
- My car is in excellent condition, and I keep it clean.
- My work environment is well organized and inspiring.
- I love all the clothes in my closet.
- My home is in good repair.
- I am living in the geographic location I want to live in.
- I love my lifestyle and the way I live my life.

Fun and Relaxation

- I have fun on a regular basis.
- I laugh freely and easily.
- I have people in my life that I can play with.
- I have activities in my life that are fun for me and I do them regularly.
- I have activities that are relaxing for me, and I do them regularly.
- I take breaks for fun and relaxation, and do not work non-stop.
- I have fun things planned in the future that I look forward to.

Chapter 16:
Mastering Yourself and Your Career

"The first and best victory is to conquer self."
– Plato

What a journey. Throughout this book, you have learned so much about yourself. On a personal note, I went through a healing process. When I woke up this morning, I prayed and meditated and asked what the close of this book should be. Within two hours, three things were revealed, to me, for you.

- First of all, be grateful and trust. You're blessed by your ability to wake up each morning. Focusing on what's in front of you first is the most critical step forward.
- You are equally as beautiful as the universe (courtesy of my Berry Detox Yogi tea).
- Joel Osteen bringing us Biblical wisdom: *"For we who have believed do enter that rest..."* (Hebrews 4:3, NKJV) God promises that there are "set times" in our future to bring His promises to pass in our lives, but He doesn't tell us when they will be. Your set time may be tomorrow

morning at 9:47." You can relax knowing there's the right time for everything, and while you wait, you can choose to do so with a good attitude.

You now understand how all parts of life influence your higher purpose, which is to be your true self. By now, you should have completed a career plan that's ready to be loved and embraced! But you've gained so much more! You've achieved a great understanding of your authentic self and appreciate your value, knowledge, that the way you are designed is precisely who the world needs. You have learned practical means of getting to know yourself, of embracing, and evolving, who you are. Using the methods learned, you can now identify gifts and talents and techniques, so that in return, you can embrace your personal growth, relationships, your health, and space. Ultimately, life is to be lived and shared.

Exercise: Take a moment to write yourself a thank you letter to yourself for completing this process, for taking time to invest in yourself, values, and position on this earth. Do so with kindness and love. It's a demonstration of your love for yourself, and will bring the most meaningful, long-lasting impact.

Integrating Career into Your Life

The process starts with you, your wheel of life, and gratitude. Although, you might have been trying to connect with the choice of career path, you've found that it starts with yourself. There's so much more to your complete self. Understanding that you have all you need to feel fulfillment, and being grateful, makes you exponentially more powerful.

Isn't it exciting to learn that your Fascination Profile is a mystique; or that your leading dosha is Vata, and so you're pure movement and air; or that you draw squiggly lines and hearts when you are bored, because you have a type of energy that's bubbly and inspiring; and that all of it is normal for you? The most amazing experience is recognizing your features make you unique. The more we try to blend in externally or belong, the more we're trying to run away from ourselves.

Your best career match is one that offers the opportunity to embrace your strengths and core values, and where you're equally equipped to share your talents and gifts. The best approach to follow your steps is genuinely to connect with your inner wisdom and Higher Power, trusting that there's a path and timing perfect for you. We are part of a much larger plan that enables each to carry out our purpose.

Prioritizing and Focus

You've learned the importance of prioritizing, and of understanding how you are indeed using your time. Each of your life components influences the other. Together they are in motion to flow and to support your path. Your ability to prioritize and focus on the elements that are valuable to you requires discipline and guidance, using yourself as your most precious asset. But for you to be at your best, your first step is to look inward. Looking inward helps us understand that we have the necessary resources to execute our talents and gifts, as long as we embrace them and kindly and compassionately share them with the rest of the world. There are times when saying "no" demonstrates your value and the limits you set for yourself. There's a season to nurture each of our priorities, as our life and your personal growth further develops.

Take a Look at Your SMART Goals

Exercise: If you refer to your original career plan, the one you wrote at the beginning of this book, you might consider making some changes based on the SMART goals. If you haven't, take a look at each of your chapter self-assessment questions or notes. Does any of it change your career plan? Readers who are most successful in executing to the plan acknowledge and embrace the notion that each area of their life influences their career, and adapt their plans throughout their lives, to ensure there's alignment with their life goals. Tracking your path while using your inner wisdom to guide your thoughts and approach will keep you on track and accountable.

Evolving – It's an Ongoing Process

Personal growth plays a crucial role in manifesting the right perspective of the world around you. Remember: It's a continuing process. Our circumstances, knowledge, intellect, and more importantly, our connection to our original design will change; we must adapt to maintain the right position and track toward the master plan. Our unique designs were given to us even before birth. Once we entered into this world, the environment and lessons from guardians or parents, siblings, and their energy started piling up to form who we are today. Identifying our core values, those that came with the original design, then became our first step. Without this step, any subsequent thought continues to use the altered version of ourselves.

Aligning our core values with our priorities builds up a plan to reflect our strengths, and where we are most needed, and this will bring satisfaction. It brings light to others, and guides your steps by inner wisdom, which is the ultimate wisdom. Unlike external knowledge that's influenced by other energies and worlds, that brings limitations and rules to how our designs should operate, inner wisdom also brings caring abundance.

Our relationship with the material world is often a significant driver of our career over our lifetimes, when, indeed, they each follow a separate path. Like any life aspect, they influence each other, but they are not the same. When we're in a position of giving, working our capital, and exerting effort proactively; then over time, your career becomes one with yourself, not with money or titles. Your identity shifts from what you do to who you are.

Connecting with the inner child helps us connect with the child that we need to nurture. It helps us to collect our thoughts and heal wounds we might have been carrying for years. Surfacing our wounds will help us to continuously evolve and connect to our inner wisdom. Acknowledging that there's more to you, to us and the world's creations, allows you to set your ego aside to make space for your Higher Power, Your Creator, love, the universe. It's the ultimate source, the one of truth, compassion, love, dependability, and kindness. It's the one that never fails. Connecting to your source breaks through any erosion or wounds that the world may have imposed, and allows your original and one-of-a-kind design to surface.

Practicing mindfulness and exercises that connect with your chakras enable the energy from your inner space to move out into the world. You are and will continue being more careful about your time and space.

But you also recognized that we're not alone, and that we've been all created to be different. Our features are not about how we function, as we learned through Pink's work, but the value we bring into the space and outward into the world. Relationships with all living creatures are meant to establish a synchronous melody of growth, aspirations, and desire to promote a mission. When we come together, it's almost like a chorus. We each play a tune to the most inspiring song, and our growth and purpose multiples like fireworks. We light up when we lift each other, and we share love and compassion for each other, because we are designed to share and receive love. Each living creature has a place and position in this work, and it's for us to respect, honor, and esteem each one. Our relationships reflect each other like mirrors, as we're created from a single source. Authenticity becomes of the essence, as we attract who we are. Whether it is your co-workers, family, or friends, we belong to the world chorus, and together, our career serves a purpose.

Our talents and gifts were meant to be shared and contributed to our neighbors, our communities, and our world. When we become one, our purpose brings fulfillment, and it's then that we can recognize the abilities and qualities of others; giving translates to love. Love is an action that results in feelings as we process through our thoughts, and it's transmitted manifesting our attention. That's the fine line between love and fear. It's called intention.

Health keeps us alive. You are the asset; without health, there's no asset, there's no career. So it's not the act of balancing that you should seek; it's one of prioritizing, keeping in mind that these are not equal. One enables the other to exist. Maintaining mind-body-spirit health is vital; a lack of health blocks our ability to project ourselves, with authenticity, drive, and compassion. Our energies, doshas, and chakras serve as a proxy to best maintain optimal health. Each carries a momentum that fuels our mission and purpose.

Our inside world merges with our outside. The power of organizing our space allows the universe to hold and nurture us, like a baby in the arms of a loving mother. The abundance and flow of energy feeds into every particle of our essence. It manifests not only the space in our careers, but our central positions in our world. Clutter, obstacles, and difficulties should be cleared with love and gratitude. An object or relationship in our life, each serves a purpose, even if it's just for a season. Eliminating physical objects represents our ability to remove life obstacles.

Fulfillment and mission flourish by sharing our talents and gifts, or building relationships; yet ultimately, we understand that the assets – ourselves – are worthy of recreation and grounding time. During a career transition, work-life balance can be compromised. So it's vital to recognize that there's a time and a place for all of our life aspects. It's also essential to understand that work is part of life; life is not part of work. Therefore, the use of our free time is a reflection of the respect and our view of self-value. Active recreation or hobbies maintain a healthy connection with our inner wisdom, and allows us to benefit from the lightness and adventures it brings our way. Work-life balancing then becomes an act of balancing the use of all parts of our mind, body, and spirit.

Embrace your successes and learn from your failures. Remember: The best plans are those that have clear objectives, attainable, and accountable goals, as we learned through the development of SMART goals. But the most successful and achieved plans are those that are flexible with the constant shift in our environment, our personal growth, relationships, health, and space. Life is like an ocean of waves, with seasons of high and low tides, intensity, and calmness; but overall, there's no good or bad. We interpret good or bad, when things go or do not go according to plan. But our plan is just there to guide our path, not our life. The reason for this is because our paths roll up to a much higher plan that connects humanity to build and use our true authentic selves.

We each have free will, and each conscious decision will have an effect in the time and space, to the level of a molecule. This is why our thoughts, words, and actions truly matter. Our inner wisdom, then, becomes our own personal compass that guides us, once we're connected and carefully listening, allowing us to guide our steps without us trying to invade or overtake. Letting go and surrendering our egos will enable us to stay connected and master ourselves without fear, but only with love and compassion.

Finally Mastering Yourself

Today, I continue to navigate the calm and sometimes torrential waters of career development. I continue advancing my path as a healthcare thought-leader, one of empowerment and inspiration, while expanding my life coaching practice. One of the most significant challenges for me has been the volatility involved in managing a business of your own. Combine that with a young marriage, and close friends and family, and you have a busy life. It's been a journey of my own to write this book, and to trust that it lands in the hands that need it the most.

My relationships with my parents and family are much clearer these days. It's less about belonging and more about honoring and respecting them. We each have our downfalls and differences, and that doesn't translate to any of us being superior or inferior. I don't have to be right. I wouldn't change my parents for the world. Both are perfectly designed to serve as my parents, and regardless of our blind spots, they intend to give love the in ways they know.

I recognize that humanity has made significant strides towards its betterment, but I also know that we have a long way to go. I see the violence and the division that exists in our country, along with the day-to-day opportunities to be more compassionate and kinder, in our workforce, in our organizations. It remains clear to me that we must continue to find our real positions in the world. When in doubt, I start by adjusting my inner self, acknowledging that our careers, our lives go well beyond what we're able to see.

At some point, I did work hard. I now work smarter. Smarter, because I'm rowing with what seems to be more natural to me these days. Keeping my ego in check has helped during my not-so-motivated days. Get out of your head and put things into action, knowing that action alone only goes so far. When you add kindness and love into your activities, it magnifies their value. Knowing and being grateful for the wisdom that comes from the love that brought me to this earth makes a world of difference.

Your fear is a spirit, and the ego gives it a body; if you allow your thoughts, words, and actions to be driven by this source, it's like downloading incompatible software or a virus to your phone. Your phone slows down; its functionality will be compromised; its purpose will be limited. You are a much more powerful being. You carry around the tools of love and source of wisdom you need to express and live your authentic purpose. Today may be about your career, but know that you're much more than a title, an organization, or a job. You are the presence of energy that's much greater than us, of an incomprehensible loving spirit that allows us to float in this universe. We're blessed to have our relationships, our health, our space, our commodities, and to be able to share all of it is a real demonstration of love.

I'm grateful for your loving commitment to take action and embrace who you are. You are helping all of us by doing so. With me, you have a friend who loves you, honors, and admires you precisely as you were designed to be. Your career goal is indeed achieved when you realize and exercise your real purpose; and our purpose is to know, embrace, love, and share ourselves.

Today, I'd like to introduce you to a time of trust, trust that's there's more to you. Whether it's your career, your health, or your relationships, there's a story for you that's ready to take off. It starts with your humility and surrender. From now on, your days will never be the same. Each day will bring new clues, synchronicity, and affirmations that you're going on the right track. You're connected to the most loving source of wisdom, and each day, you will learn and act according to your purpose: being your true self.

Appendix

Links and Resources

- Page 51: Core Values Index: https://conscious endeavors.org/core-values-index/
- Page 55:
  - University of Pennsylvania Authentic Happiness website: https://www.authentichappiness.sas.upenn.edu/
  - VIA Institute on Character: https://www.viacharacter.org/character-strengths
- Page 59: Circle of Influence: https://www.thensomehow.com/circles-of-influence/
- Page 64: Wheel of Life: https://wheeloflife.noomii.com/
- Page 69: The Life Path: https://seventhlifepath.com/
- Page 73: Vision board: https://www.makeavisionboard.com/what-is-a-vision-board/
- Page 94:
  - Occupational Information Network: https://www.onetonline.org/
  - Occupational Outlook Handbook: https://www.bls.gov/ooh/
- Page 95:
  - GradSquare: http://www.gradsquare.com/home
  - Linked In: https://www.linkedin.com/
- Page 99: Fascination Advantages: https://www.howtofascinate.com/

- Page 101: https://www.innerbonding.com/show-page/203/learn-inner-bonding-now.html
- Page 105: Carol Tuttle's Energy Profile: https://my.live yourtruth.com/dyt/profiling-tool/
- Page 114: Frameworks: https://myframeworks.org/emotional-intelligence-tools/
- Page 133: Osho's website: https://www.osho.com/read/osho/osho-on-topics/love
- Page 138: Chakras: https://manifestsmagic.com/7-chakras-unlock-all-7-chakras/
- Page 168: Love Language Quiz: https://www.5love languages.com/quizzes/
- Page 176: Critters in the cube farm: perceived psychological and organizational effects of pets in the workplace Study: https://www.ncbi.nlm.nih.gov/pubmed/11199259
- Page 193: Dosha Type Quiz: https://shop.chopra.com/dosha-quiz/
- Page 194: Chopra Center website: https://chopra.com/
- Page 197: Downshiftology website: https://down shiftology.com/
- Page 203: Performing a body scan: https://www.mindful.org/beginners-body-scan-meditation/
- Page 206: Yoga Journal: https://www.yogajournal.com/practice/beginners-guide-chakras
- Page 216: Squirrels of a Feather: https://www.squirrel sofafeather.com/
- Page 217: The Spruce: https://www.thespruce.com/
- Page 218: Feng Shui Octagon: https://feng-shui.loveto know.com/Bagua_Octagon

33 Daily Lessons to Master Yourself

A master is not a master over others, but of yourself. Is having an awareness of your inner source, not of the outside. There's nothing more liberating than knowing you are the master of your destiny. Integrate into your daily routine on any and all areas of your life as you move along getting to know yourself a little better each day.

- Day 1 - Compromise: Confusion is the start of your journey, as you become more familiar with yourself, the more the ego will try to convince of what's rational. Continue your path forward, don't try to find a compromise between your past and where you're going. You'll remain the same and not change.

- Day 2 - Sorrow: Pain is there to alert you, not to cause sadness. Times of sorrow has a high potential for transformation. But one must go deep down to understand the root while nurturing oneself and seeing the opportunity for the change.

- Day 3- Be the fool: Following your intuition, your heart and trust may seem foolish to some. But it's the only way to live in the present and build out your purpose.

- Day 4 - The Fight: Are you exhausted from working so hard? Trying to stay positive, but deep down, you seem to be resistance. It might be time to put your mask and armor down. It's ok to uncover your wound and let healing begin. There's so much love available to you. Fight the flight of love, you're worthy of it.

- Day 5 - Experience a tree: Have you ever hugged a tree before? Try it. Nature is mindless. We may think of humans as the most intelligent species, but nature always has a way of getting it consistently right. Take it the seasons, the cycle of its ecosystem. The universe is there for you, not against you. Let it whisper, let it hug, and nurture you.

- Day 6 - The Burden: We live in lies, our own, and others. We all have dreams and our path to conquer, but without releasing the masks and expectations imposed by ourselves and others, we will never have the energy to reach them. You and your experiences, along with your expectations, have different lanes. Stay on your path.

- Day 7 - The Past: The past no longer exists. Our memories of our past are only there to remind us of our repeated journeys. It is a proxy and opportunity for healing, not an indicator of our future.

- Day 8 - Harmony: Listening to our hearts is freedom. To follow our beats, expressing ourselves from a source of love. Using ourselves as designed, not how others would like us to throb. It's when we reach a place that we enjoy our foolishness, playfulness, and personal charm and drop worldly rhymes.

- Day 9 - Patience: Sometimes, it's as simple as waiting. Like a beautiful pregnant woman, without a trace of stress and anxiety. She knows the day will come. We're designed perfectly to dance with space and time. Patience will allow us to enjoy our playgrounds while we wait, trusting it's there for you, even better than what you'd imagine or can envision.

- Day 10 - Participation: You're a participant in a story much more significant than yourself. Acknowledging this notion, helps you go through the motion of not always liking what's happening, but grounding you to the level of only performing according to yourself – your most meaningful contribution of all.

- Day 11 - Beyond Your Limitations: Humans are limited to our experience and external knowledge. Looking inward will help us understand our mission. Look passed your judgment, expectations, and past behavior.

- Day 12 - Change: It is continuous and constant. Resisting it causes the universe to take matters into its own hands. Like a cyclone, move towards the center of it, and you'll lessen the turmoil. You'll come out stronger to admire the rainbows afterward.

- Day 13 - Chaos: If your world seems shaky right now, know that opposites forces are life's cycle. There's sunshine after a storm; after a fire, the earth is replenished. You must detach from the feeling of chaos, as you both have separate paths. Accept each circumstance, and feel the opportunity for change and love.

- Day 14 - Innocence: It's the beauty of a child. Connecting with your inner child allows the intent for playfulness and joy before being conditioned with expectations and external behavior. It nourishes you with the plentifulness to respond to this ever-changing world and external hardships.

- Day 15 - Letting go: Maybe bring sorrow and fear, but it represents liberation and freedom. Allow one season to go and another to start – your identity to be used and satisfied for one phase and a leap of faith to the unknown, whether it is your career, relationship, or your physical space. Letting go welcomes the greatness that awaits you and move away from what has previously defined you.

- Day 16 - Suppression: Don't feel like a bird in a cage. Let all of it out. Expression and reveals allows for healing. Without it, you're preparing for an explosion. The universe always has a way of compensating to meet the broader mission, whether you are ready or not.

- Day 17 - Abundance: You have more than what you're capable of understanding. Start acting like it: yourself, your inner wisdom, your relationships. Your mere presence and your contributions as your authentic self, make the world. You will never be left empty-handed because you're the only capable of depleting yourself from your born gifted goods.

- Day 18 - Your external child: Out thoughts often keep replaying with issues and words from the past. The voice convinces and torments you with the ideas, that you're not enough or the many imperfections you've convinced yourself as having.

Instead, connect with your inner child, forgive, forget, and nourish it.

- Day 19 - The Source: It's your center, your grounds of love and nourishment. Whether you are at peace, going through hard times, or just enjoying a day at the beach, take the team to connect. It will help you stay centered and right to yourself regardless of the rain, cloudy, or sunny days ahead.

- Day 20 - Sharing: You're in a position of sharing your love, joy, and care. There so much abundance that it's overflowing all over you. Stay centered and give at every opportunity. The universe will pour you with laughter and celebrations.

- Day 21 - Transformation: it's beauty and is consistent with the patters of the universe and the constant change that occurs around you. Transformation gives birth to opportunities and end to past events. It's time to let go and accept newness. It comes at the right time with ease of movement. Take the time to be silenced to listen to the waves of motion being brought to you. Be patient.

- Day 22 - Intensity: Move with energy, confidence, and fire. Not fear and intimidation. You are invisible. You may seem different to others. Whether they like it or not, is irrelevant. Know that your spirit will get you exactly where you need to go.

- Day 23 - Laziness: Your sense of complacency may have originated from a place of achievement, and it feels like drinking marshmallow cocoa on a crisp winter day. Don't fall for it.

Letting go involves leaving your results behind. Don't look back, only forward. It's tempting to slow down now, but this is not the end of your journey. There's much exploring to do ahead.

- Day 24 - The Miser: Don't hold on to your possessions. The dollars in your bank, even the people around you, nothing belongs to you. Only your love and connection to your inner source exists. Whatever you're holding onto, let it go and allow the abundance and freedom that comes with sharing.

- Day 25 - Inner Voice: It's the loving voice that uses no words. It connects with you through silence and only speaks that language of your heart. In our world, too much information and views pull us in different directions. If you're confused, it's time to be centered in silence. The inner voice will come through with clarity and nourishment.

- Day 26 - The Creator: He welcomes you with joy to participate in the broader mission. No limitations, just abundance. Connecting with it allows you to tap into beyond desired gifts and talents. His contributions are perfectly designed for you with creativity and love. Using them will enable you to open new stages of your life.

- Day 27 - Celebration: There are moments to celebrate every day! Don't wait for the big holiday party. Celebrate and be grateful for all that you have available to you; Your health, relationships, your material goods that provide you convenience and security. Opening yourself to celebrations will lead to more significant opportunities to celebrate. Share the beauty with others! It's contagious.

- Day 28 - Breakthrough: There are times when enough is enough. If that's the case for you, take the leap of faith and confront your greatest fears and move past a life of limitations and old behavior. Welcome the opportunities to explore new horizons and moments of joy.

- Day 29 - Crying: It brings healing. Open yourself to feeling the feelings. We're often taught to toughen up and put up the mask to be politically correct. There's nothing pretty about politics. Drop fallacies and welcome resources and love that will help you heal.

- Day 30 - Consciousness: You are positioned to be a whole. There's beauty that comes without being aware that your wisdom is coming from the source of love, from your inner self, not the mind. Know that you are potent, stable, and your existence is all there is to you. Enjoy and share this knowledge.

- Day 31 - Success: It's a result of efforts, failures, and experience. The highest wisdom of all is to know that whether they be valleys or peaks, is that "this too will pass." Enjoy the moment and celebrate, including the journey that helps you reach this moment.

- Day 32 - Projections: Be clear about your core values and beliefs. Don't be blinded by others' feelings or thoughts. Don't let others influence or blur your vision. Each of us carries and responsible for our paths and journey.

- Day 33 - Existence: "Home" is not a real place in the outside world, but an inner quality of relaxation and acceptance. Feeling at home, with all masks down, naked in the sense of purpose allows you to see things for what they are, in their pure state, no judgment, no pain. Spend time with nature, and you'll notice how much at home each star in the sky, and the wind as it flows the leafy trees at the park.

Acknowledgments

I'm blessed to have so many of you as my life soul family. It's the most loving and nurturing village one can have!

I want to first thank my loving husband Mark. You bring out playful butterflies and authenticity in me. You inspired me to share with others what it means to be re-al-deal and truly love. Thanks for your encouragement and sneaking in fun time in the middle of wedding planning and book writing. You were as essential to writing this book as I was. Thanks for sharing this special milestone and life with me.

To my dog Luna for keeping my feet warm as I was writing, every single day. Her belly rubs and sweet eyes reminded me that there's love in everything and everyone.

To my mom, Nicolasina, and dad, Julio, whom I love dearly. They will forever be the start of my journey and I'm grateful for their love and dedication to raising a loving family.

To my sister, Carolina, brother in law-Josh, and my awesome nephews, Christian and Jeremy. Thanks for your presence, love and care through such a long journey. You're core to my life and aspirations.

To my best friend, sister-from-another-mother, Karina. You rock my world! You are the spark that ignites so many of our lives and certainly mine. Thank you for being my soundboard and a lifeline for so many years.

To my best friend, soul sister, Juana. Thank you for introducing me to life and adventure. You're the original and only unicorn, giving your rainbows and fairy dust to everyone around you.

To my new family, who's welcomed me with open arms and hearts, Joan, Mike, Alexis, Matt, Linsley, Freddy, Chase and Reigen. Thanks for sharing Markie with me and being so loving and giving!

To my group of strong women and mentors, who's spiritual job is to inspire and love, Toni, Jenny, Karen, and Tracy. Thank you for going beyond your call of duty to inspire and give so much of yourself each day.

To my spiritual and physical support Mariola, Monika, Avalon, and Marine. Thanks for keeping my spirit and body on point!

To my family at Mont Lawn City Camp. What an amazing group of souls! Thanks for building a community for our kids and the mentors that are blessed to participate in the program.

To my team at work, you will forever be my family. Thanks for trusting me with your careers and jobs. You're the most talented group of individuals I've ever met. Thanks for allowing me part of your lives.

Each one of you has given me the opportunity to look inward and to love myself that much more. Thanks for being you.

About the Author

Vanessa Guzman-Schepis is in an award-winning healthcare executive, thought-leader, and life coach. She develops and oversees corporate visions and creates sustainable roadmaps to success. After over a decade of leading initiatives that promote healthcare delivery and efficiency, she realized that real transformation occurs when one empowers individuals and communities.

Vanessa became a life coach in 2013. Since then, Vanessa has been able to combine her technical and healthcare expertise to develop a program called SmartRise System. The program walks individuals through key life components to build a customized plan that helps them reach their goals and live right to their purpose. Through one-on-one sessions, she helps clients implement an individualized plan.

Vanessa is a native New Yorker, first-generation from loving Dominican parents. She has lived through what she describes as "dual-worlds", often trying to meet the demands that come with being raised in a Hispanic household underserved community and transitioning to life in America. Her life experience encouraged her to set a path of limitless possibilities for herself and others.

Vanessa graduated from Columbia University with Bachelor of Science and a Master of Science degrees in Biomedical Engineering. She was raised in a culturally loyal, traditional home, a world that subjected women to a secondary role, with predestined life outcomes as an adult. But Vanessa always knew there was more, and since then has been an advocate of community enrichment and growth.

One of Vanessa's most heart-felt passions is being a mentor volunteer at the Bowery Mission's Mont Lawn City Camp Leadership Academy. Mont Lawn City Camp serves more than 250 children each year from low-income families in the South Bronx and East Harlem neighborhoods of NYC.

Vanessa lives with her loving and witty husband Mark, and her human-spirited dog Luna, in Brooklyn,

NY. Vanessa loves painting, reading and spending time in nature. Vanessa believes that everyone is in a position to be the change, starting with themselves. Vanessa sees life as a gift and life's purpose to be and to love yourself.

Email: vanessa@smartrisesolutions.com

Facebook: https://www.facebook.com/vanessa.smartrise solutions

Twitter: www.twitter.com/lifeisbliss10

Instagram: www.instagram.com/rising.and.thriving/

Website: https://www.smartrisesolutions.com/getstarted

Thank You for Reading!

Thanks so much for sharing your love for life.

I'm super grateful that you took the time to read *There's More to You: Your Career Unveiled – 10 Essential Strategies to Master Your Career, Business, and Life!* Writing this book is my world in the making. Regardless of your circumstances and how you feel today, you have taken a meaningful step. I know you have something special ticking inside in the process of being unleashed!

As a little token of love and appreciation, I'd like to offer a free thirty-minute chat! I'd love to get to know you, answer any burning questions you might have, and help you master your career plan to freedom, love, and purpose. You can schedule or stay in touch connect with me through:

Email: vanessa@smartrisesolutions.com

Facebook: https://www.facebook.com/vanessa.smartrise solutions

Twitter: www.twitter.com/lifeisbliss10

Instagram: www.instagram.com/rising.and.thriving/

Website: https://www.smartrisesolutions.com/getstarted for more resources and blogs.

Part of the revenue generated from this book and other SmartRise programs go toward children's and women empowerment and enrichment programs. Thank you for allowing me the opportunity to give to you and others.

With love and light,
Vanessa

Made in the USA
Monee, IL
02 July 2020